MW00615453

Daisy:

A Servant at Heart

Daisy:

A

Servant

at Heart

by Virginia Wright

Copyright © 1993 by Wesley Press
All Rights Reserved
Published By Wesley Press
Indianapolis, Indiana 46250
Printed in the United States of America
ISBN 0-89827-107-X

All scripture quotations, unless indicated, are taken from the HOLY
BIBLE, NEW INTERNATIONAL VERSION ® Copyright © 1973, 1978,
1984 by International Bible Society. Used by permission of Zondervan
Publishing House. All rights reserved.

Scripture quotations marked (KJV) are taken from the HOLY BIBLE,
KING JAMES VERSION.

Table of Contents

Preface

We walked around the furniture store together, Aunt Daisy and I, looking for just the right piece to place in our "new" home in Indianapolis. She was delighted with the store's charming room arrangements and stopped to touch the lovely fabrics and the rich finishes on the tables and china cabinets. Aunt Daisy could spot quality wood products with the experienced eye of the daughter of a master carpenter and cabinetmaker. Finally, we found a small buffet/server which might be what we needed in our dining room.

We agreed that it would match our dining room furniture nicely, but I wasn't sure it was the right size. I moaned at my lack of foresight, "Why didn't I bring my tape measure along?"

With a little smile and a twinkle in her eye, she said, "No problem! I brought mine just in case. And I also measured the wall space where this will go," That was Aunt Daisy! Always thinking ahead, always interested in what concerned those dear to her, always careful and precise.

Almost sixty years before our shopping excursion, she recorded her first train trip from California to Mexico in minute detail.

> *11:20. Just passed through 3rd tunnel; 11:25, the fourth; 11:40, back in the USA again. The porter just informed me that we are to pass through 17 tunnels in a stretch, soon. Here is the first! These mountains are solid rock piles, barren and hot. We went through all 17 (only I counted 19). One took us 90 seconds to go through!*

That trip to Mexico launched a missionary career for Daisy Elizabeth Buby that began on July 20, 1928. It spanned forty-nine years of service in five countries, including deputation (according to Aunt Daisy, not so exciting as actual missionary service, but almost), and nine years given in loving care of her invalid parents. It included visits to many other lands where her prayers and sacrificial offerings were invested and where her world view demanded that she see for herself what the Lord was doing.

She retired three times, the third and final retirement coming in 1977. Even after that, her conversations centered around what she lovingly called "the work," and were sprinkled with the names and activities of her missionary colleagues and friends old and new. She never turned down an opportunity to participate in a missionary service, speaking twice during the last month of her life. She was still a missionary at heart, living and breathing missions until the day of her death, October 25, 1987.

. . . .

When I told Aunt Daisy that I had been asked to write a book about her, she was utterly amazed that anyone would consider her life to be "book material." Her immediate response was, "Surely not me!"

After some hesitation, Aunt Daisy agreed to permit this book to be written, and eagerly began the process of gathering information together and making her diaries, journals, and correspondence available to me for the project. She came from her retirement home in Brooksville, Florida, to spend a few weeks with us and to tell me her life story.

We had hardly begun when it was time for her to return to Brooksville. She promised to continue recording information for me on cassette, but her ailing heart began to give her trouble the day after she arrived home. Ten days later, God took her home. I was left to search through the volumes of material which Daisy Buby wrote through the years. I found the incredibly detailed chronicles of her life fascinating and revealing.

The words of a song on the flyleaf of one of her Bibles reveal the secret of her selfless life. It must have been her constant prayer.

> *Oh, to be like Thee! Oh, to be like Thee,*
> *Blessed Redeemer, pure as Thou art!*
> *Come in Thy sweetness, come in Thy fulness;*
> *Stamp Thine own image deep on my heart.*

> *Thomas O. Chisholm*

In the pages which follow, I have attempted to tell her story, to record some of the significant events of the rich, full life of this missionary saint who bore the "servant" image of her Lord with dignity and grace.

Virginia Wright

Acknowledgments

*T*his book could never have been written without the help of several important people in my life. First of all, I am indebted to Aunt Daisy herself who entrusted her diaries, letters, and journals to me even before God took her home. This book came from those thousands of pages written by her own hand. I have striven to be faithful to her record of her own life.

I am grateful to my husband who became a patient sounding board for the interesting "finds" in Aunt Daisy's letters and journals. He gave invaluable suggestions as the writing progressed, and encouragement when heavy travel schedules at home and overseas interrupted the "flow" of the work. He believed in me and the project even when I nearly gave up in despair.

My dear friend, Phyllis Ihrkey Mitchell, edited the manuscript and gave suggestions as to format and style. My son, Dr. David Wright, critiqued my first faltering beginnings on this book and helped me focus the vast store of material from which I have told Aunt Daisy's story. My daughter, Mrs. Beth Fussner, read the manuscript and gave suggestions which made the project easier.

Together, we give the book to you with the prayer that "Aunt Daisy" will continue to live on and influence your life through these pages.

Part I

The Early Years
A Missionary in the Making

"When God wants to do His great works, He trains somebody to be quiet enough and little enough, then He uses that person."

Hudson Taylor

Chapter 1

Spiritual Foundations

God Speaks, Daisy Listens

The word of the Lord came to me, saying, "Before I formed you in the womb I knew you, before you were born I set you apart; I appointed you . . ." (Jeremiah 1:4-5 NIV).

The dawning of the twentieth century was filled with the splendor of expectancy for William and Bessie Buby. Their first child was to be born in May of 1900. The coming of spring intensified their anticipation as they watched nature break out of the dreary chrysalis of winter. Would it be a boy? Would it be a girl? What would this child become? Filled with the awesome wonder of being partners with God in His creative processes, they dedicated their unborn child to the purposes He had in mind.

They welcomed Daisy Elizabeth Buby (pronounced Beuby) to their home in Burnside, Michigan, on May 10, 1900. Less than two weeks later they took her to church, because that was their habit and because they realized their profound responsibility to raise this child for God. It didn't matter that there was no junior church or nursery, or that babies cried and children whispered and squirmed in their seats. Church was the center of the family's spiritual and social life. William and Bessie attended every service and gave many happy hours to its various activities.

Daisy's concept of serving God was shaped in a home where religion was more than a "going to church" affair. It was an intensely practical, every day matter. It meant participating in family worship when their father read from the large Bible and prayed for each of his children by name. Many times, she heard the pronouncements, "It is a sin to tell a lie, and to steal. And if we tell lies and steal, we need to ask Jesus to forgive us."

Daisy remembered how she and Alvin, her younger brother, got into mischief. She was eight years old and he was six. Her tender conscience troubled her until she persuaded Alvin that they must ask Jesus to forgive them. Together they knelt beside her bed and prayed as they had heard others do until they felt at peace again.

Daisy's "Papa" was a builder who prided himself on meticulous, careful work. He delighted in creating lovely furniture and buildings from fine wood. His trade took him and his family from Burnside to San Diego, California, by way of Greeley, Colorado.

The five-year sojourn in Greeley was significant for the Buby family. Here their search for a Bible-believing fellowship like the German Methodist Church they had left behind in Michigan led them to the Church of the Nazarene. Daisy gave her heart to Jesus in a children's meeting there at the age of twelve. In the testimony she wrote on her application for missionary service many years later, she described how she tried to tell a classmate about her wonderful experience. She said, "I started out being a missionary the very next morning."

"The whole world seemed new. How beautiful the stars! How bright the moon! How green and pretty the trees. I tried to testify to a friend in school the next day, but it was all a foreign language to her, so with tears I said, 'You will just have to come to my church and find out.'"

The move to California came a year later. Papa Buby's fame as a carpenter and contractor reached San Diego, where he was offered the opportunity to help construct the buildings for the great Pan American Exposition of 1915. After five years, it was difficult to leave the beautiful home William had built for his family. Leaving the loving, vibrant church family was even harder, but the exciting work offer and the news that there was a strong Nazarene church in San Diego gave them courage to make the move.

The Bubys quickly became a part of the Church of the Nazarene in San Diego and made themselves almost indispensable. The children attended the Christian grammar school operated by the church. It was there that Daisy began to learn about sanctification. The pastor taught that the holy life which began when one was forgiven for his sins continued until a second work of grace took place. That was when the Christian asked God to fill him with the Holy Spirit and to cleanse his nature in response to complete surrender of himself to God. He called it being sanctified. Like a flower opening its petals under the warmth and light of the sun, Daisy responded to the teaching, and by her own testimony, was sanctified in the fall of 1913.

She learned that living the "sanctified" life day by day meant giving up her own way sometimes. One of those challenges came on an exciting missionary Sunday at their church. All during the morning service, Daisy was wide-eyed with wonder as the missionaries told fascinating stories of other lands and people.

Daisy and Alvin shared the responsibility of taking their little sister and baby brother home from morning service. They were to feed and put them to bed for their afternoon naps. The rest of the family including Nelson, the middle child, remained for the afternoon Bible studies and children's meeting.

"It's your turn to take Elva and Billy home today," Alvin reminded Daisy with a smug smile.

"Is it? But I wanted to stay for the afternoon this time," responded Daisy. After a moment of hesitation, she continued with quiet resignation, "I wanted to hear the missionaries again, but it is my turn. I'll go."

After Daisy reached home and performed her duties for the children, she faced the long, boring afternoon that stretched out ahead of her. Several delightful activities popped into her head, some forbidden on Sundays, but tempting since she was being denied the joy of being at church. It didn't seem fair that she had to stay at home while the rest of the family enjoyed the special meetings. Daisy's own heart inclinations and careful home training in "proper Sunday afternoon behavior" conquered those temptations to become involved in frivolous pursuits. She tried to read her Bible, but her concentration was broken again and again by the images and ideas impressed on her mind that morning in the missionary service.

All at once, her reverie was interrupted by an almost-audible voice which distinctly asked the question, "Would you like to be a missionary?"

"Where did that voice come from?" Daisy questioned her sanity for a moment as she glanced around the room for the speaker. Again the question was asked, not a demand but an invitation, for Daisy was not the kind of child who needed to be coerced. "Would you like to be a missionary?"

When she became certain that it was God speaking, she knelt at the chair and began to talk it over with Him. She committed the rest of her life to God to be His messenger that afternoon, adding a special request to her consecration, "And please don't let anything or anyone cause me to deviate from your

will." At fourteen, Daisy had no idea what things and people
would come along to test that consecration. She only knew that
she could hardly wait for her parents to come home.

God's call and Daisy's response turned the house upside
down that Sunday, March 8, 1914, in the quiet intense way the
Buby household could be turned upside down. This was not a
family accustomed to hysterical demonstrations of either sorrow
or joy. It was a quiet, controlled, disciplined home where feelings ran deeply and found expression in logical, well-mannered
actions. Daisy's announcement was made with twinkling blue
eyes blazing with certainty, as a heavenly smile lighted her
pleasant round face. She declared her intentions with the finali-
ty of one who was all but in India already, explaining that was
where she was certain she should go as a missionary nurse.

Papa Buby assured her of his undying support through every
step of preparation and service. Mama Buby cried for joy all the
rest of the day that God had honored them by calling their
daughter into His work. She also cried for sorrow that one day
this delight of her heart, her willing helper, would leave home.
India seemed very far away and almost unreachable in 1914, and
her "child" seemed very young to be so sure. But if Daisy
thought she was called to India, then India it would be!

Papa and Mama Buby were not surprised that God had chosen Daisy for His work, because they had known there was
something special about this child even before she was born.
They felt a great wonder that God had pulled back the curtain of
Daisy's life for a little glimpse into her future. How marvelous to
have it stretching out before her, already placed in the hands of
their loving Heavenly Father!

God was at work several generations before her parents to
prepare the environment in which Daisy was to grow. Her great-
grandparents and grandparents were devoted Christians, having
come to know the Lord early in life. Her great-grandparents
came from Germany in the early 1800s and brought their strong
faith with them. Grandfather Buby, following in his father's
footsteps in the German Methodist Church, declared that he
wanted all of his children and grandchildren to become
Christians and to be called of the Lord. His prayer that God
would call Christian workers from his family was answered in
several of his grandchildren, including Daisy.

Throughout her early teen years, the spiritual life of her
church and school reinforced her home training and kept the
challenge of Christian service constantly before her. Special rallies
and missionary meetings were a frequent part of the program,

meetings in which the visiting missionaries all seemed to be from India or Africa. She didn't know one could be a missionary anywhere else in the world. That is why she had chosen India when God called her that March Sunday afternoon.

Why a missionary nurse? Because her tender heart was broken as she listened to the missionaries' stories about the great physical needs of the people. The logical conclusion was that God wanted her to be a nurse. She did become a nurse, and although she used her nursing skills throughout her life, nursing was not her primary work on the mission fields where she served. And she only reached India as a visitor after her missionary career was finished!

Many years later, her own words put those "logical" conclusions into perspective. "How we do like to help the Lord out!"

Chapter 2

Personal Disciplines

School Days and Delays

Wait for the Lord; be strong and take heart and wait for the Lord (Psalm 27:14 NIV).

The First Nazarene Church was filled with happy families on graduation day, June 10, 1915. Among them were Daisy's Mama, Papa, and her brothers and sisters all smiling proudly as Daisy stood behind the pulpit to deliver her graduation address. Because she finished "grammar" school at the Nazarene Christian School at the top of the class, she was chosen to give the student address at the graduation ceremonies. The theme paragraph from that oration reveals unusual maturity and understanding of moral values for a fifteen-year-old.

> *It is moral courage that characterizes the highest order of manhood and womanhood — the courage to seek and speak the truth, the courage to be just, the courage to be honest, to resist temptation, to do one's duty.*

After that, Daisy took only an occasional high school class at the church school until 1917. That was a turning-point year in Daisy's life, because it was an epochal year in the Nazarene church in southern California. Seth C. Rees, the dynamic pastor of the University Church of the Nazarene in Pasadena, and Dr. H. Orton Wiley, president of the nearby Nazarene University, were great friends and co-workers. Opposition to the leadership of these two men developed at the school, resulting in Wiley's resignation.

Subsequently, controversy swirled around Seth Rees's dynamic, fiery ministry in the church which led to the excommunication of both pastor and church by the district leadership.

After waiting for several months for some action by the denomi-
national leaders to change the previous decision, Seth C. Rees
and his congregation organized their own church. They called it
The Pilgrim Tabernacle. Other groups in California and Texas
joined with Seth Rees to form new congregations, naming this
fledgling denomination, The Pilgrim Church.

Like thousands of others, Daisy and her family were influ-
enced by the dynamic spiritual power of Seth C. Rees. Who
could forget that large impressive figure, clear brown eyes, and
huge shock of graying hair? The long-tailed frock coat flying out
behind him as he paced back and forth across the platform
made him even more unforgettable. Oratory poured from the
burning heart and keen mind of this prophet of God. Very few
who listened to the rise and fall of the musical Quaker cadence
could escape the searching, penetrating truth delivered under
the anointing of the Holy Spirit.

The Buby family left the Nazarene church and became charter members of the new Pilgrim church which was organized in
San Diego in 1917. And when Seth Rees announced the opening of Pilgrim Bible College in the fall of 1917, Daisy packed her
suitcase and went off to enroll in the high school department.

Daisy's diaries record almost daily references to Seth Rees's
challenges to holy living and complete surrender to the will of
God. They molded and shaped a lifetime of service for her. His
heart burned for missionary work abroad and at home. Again
and again, she heard him thunder, "A holiness which is not missionary is bogus." Each ringing missionary message only served
to reinforce her commitment. They called it "driving a stake" in
those days.

Sometimes the thundering tones mellowed in gentle, confi-
dence-building messages. "If you smile through your tears, they
will crystallize and adorn your crown forever."

Sometimes they pointed the way to victory over obstacles.
"He who sends us against brazen walls will be there to batter
them down."

Sometimes they contained practical advice. "If you lend
your ears to tattlers, they will come home badly soiled."

Daisy was being armed with a philosophy and a faith in God
which would carry her through many years of battle victoriously. Character qualities, already planted and growing, became
the warp and woof of her life.

Seth Rees's exhortations to punctuality, his insistence on
faithfulness to schedules and obligations reinforced the lessons
she had learned at home. One of her father's strongly enforced

dictums was, "Better to be thirty minutes early than to be one minute late!" Students dared not be late for chapel or class, lest they be lectured on the virtues of promptness.

Living in the large three-story frame building which housed dorms, dining room, library, and classrooms demanded patience and unquestioning adherence to school regulations. Strict rules governed relationships between the men and women in the school, while observance of regular study hours and participation in prayer meetings and church services were expected. While some students grumbled about the strict rules and the dorm food, she took her scheduled turn at cooking, cleaning, and serving in the dining room without complaint.

During that first year at Pilgrim Bible School, another giant Christian came marching into Daisy's life. In the spring of that year Daisy went to live and work in a nearby home for room and board. Francisco Soltero, an older Mexican student, was also living in that home. He was a ministerial student in the college program preparing to return to his own country as a missionary.

Daisy was fascinated by the stories this athletic, handsome, blue-eyed Mexican told of his homeland. She learned that he had given up a career in baseball to become a missionary. She also learned about his romance with Nettie Winans, a teacher far away in a Kansas Bible school. It made her friendship with Nettie's sister, who was a member of Pilgrim Tabernacle, even more delightful.

Francisco's Mexico captured Daisy's heart, and she could hardly wait to meet Nettie, the young woman who was willing to go there with him. The end of the school year finally arrived. Francisco graduated, married Nettie, and began his ministry in New Mexico while waiting to go to Mexico. Daisy went home to San Diego.

That summer vacation from school stretched into an interminable interlude of two and a half years, and threatened to detour Daisy from her dream of missionary nursing. The First World War was coming to a close, times were hard, and money was scarce. Daisy was keenly disappointed at the interruption, because she longed to finish high school and get on with nurses training and missionary life. Her cherished classmates and friends in Pasadena, some younger and some older than she, were painfully absent from her life. One poignant word appears again and again in her diary, "Lonesome."

Prolific letter-writing began during those years which eventually developed into a "Round Robin" that flew all over the world for more than half a century. Nearly all of her classmates and friends became missionaries and Christian workers. It was their way of giving each other detailed accounts of their activities and caring for one another through good and bad times.

Very little excitement came along during those years to punctuate the otherwise drab routine of humdrum activities. In addition to housekeeping, there were chores to perform on the small Buby acreage at the edge of San Diego. Daisy's special assignments were milking the cow and feeding the chickens. If they were especially irksome to her, her diary never recorded that fact. Sometimes she came to the end of the day "just too tired to do anything but tumble into bed."

Daisy's mind and hands were not meant to be idle either by nature or training, so she decided to take sewing and millinery courses by correspondence. And in order to forge ahead toward the mission field in spite of the delay in formal schooling, she took practical nursing courses at the community college in San Diego. Her gentle, acquiescent smile cloaked incredible tenacity. Daisy knew what God wanted her to do, and she was determined to do it in spite of all hindrances!

That training combined with Daisy's maturity and thoughtfulness opened many doors of service for her. She was called to care for sick folks, mothers and their newborn babies, and elderly people who needed nursing care. She said of some of these jobs, "And they even paid me well." Sometimes it was $1.00 a day, sometimes as much as $5.00 for a whole week of day and night duty! It seemed to Daisy that God was blessing her with a rich gold mine of possibilities as the dollars began to add up.

It wasn't all work and no play for Daisy during those years. Church activities, special meetings, and outings with a host of church friends helped to fill her days. The Buby house was headquarters for young people and adults alike who needed comfort and companionship. Everyone enjoyed Papa Buby's keen sense of humor and Mama Buby's delicious cooking and loving mothering. Daisy was a natural organizer, planning trips to the beach or picnics at the various parks in the area for her own family and church friends.

One special young man who came often kept Daisy smiling and looking ahead. A delicate thread of romance wove its way through the weeks and months, sometimes threatening to undo all her resolve to be a missionary nurse. Not long after Daisy arrived at home from that first year in Pasadena, a new pastor came to their church, accompanied by his nephew. Because the Buby family was one of the most faithful and helpful in the church, a strong friendship was formed between the pastoral family and the Bubys. It was obvious that the pastor's nephew enjoyed Daisy's company more than anyone else's in the family.

Daisy, so faithful and active in the church, so devoted to the Lord, and so diligent in her work, seemed to be an ideal find for the eligible bachelor nephew. Who could blame him for noticing the glowing winsome face lit with a happy smile, the clear blue eyes dancing with humor and goodness? Who could blame her for responding to the attention with special care to dress herself in her nicest clothing and to arrange her long shining light brown hair in her most becoming style? Who could blame her if she prayed that he would be "called" too. And who could blame the pastor and his wife for encouraging the relationship with as many encounters as they could arrange without being too obvious?

Daisy struggled with conflicting feelings of commitment to her missionary call and the desire for love and a home of her own. Very discreet notations in Daisy's diary reveal the feelings she struggled with as the friendship progressed.

> *The plot thickens.*
> *Patience is my motto.*
> *Teasing.*
> *Prayed a long time.*
> *Went to the pastor's for dinner. "He" took a picture of me and then we went on an outing.*

A very big hole was left in Daisy's life when the pastor's nephew moved away to another state. She began to watch for the mail, and tried not to show her excitement when a letter arrived for her in his handwriting.

> *I received my first letter from a young gentleman. I'm almost 20, and I "have sense!"*

Time and distance eventually dimmed the excitement of romance and strengthened her resolve to follow her God-given dream. Her attention was again focused on working and saving so that she could go back to school.

A very significant surprise came along in the fall of 1919 which brightened the long interlude at home and made her even more determined to be true to her call. Francisco and Nettie Soltero came for an extended visit. They were challenged by Seth Rees to begin work in Mexico under the banner of The Pilgrim Church, promising support for them and their ministry.

Their assignment included touring the churches of southern California to present their burden for Mexico, and to raise money for the venture.

Daisy was deeply moved by their commitment, and she was not disappointed in the young woman she had idolized from a distance. They formed a strong older-sister-younger-sister bond during subsequent weeks that lasted throughout Nettie's lifetime.

Francisco and Nettie finished their special meetings and went to Mexico in January 1920. Daisy eagerly looked forward to Nettie's frequent letters filled with accounts of the journey to Mexico, the beginning of the first church, their first convert, and their first Bible school begun in their own kitchen. The fascinating stories fed Daisy's growing interest in Mexico.

The final delay in returning to school came that fall, when once again she had to give up her dream for the sake of others. She was asked to manage the household while her mother and "little" sister went back to Michigan for a three-month visit to loved ones. She worked through the monotony of keeping the home going for her father and three brothers with dogged practicality.

> *There is a great deal of responsibility resting on my young shoulders. Yet I think that this training will help more in making a lady of me than anything.*

When Mama Buby returned from the long journey, she went immediately into the city and bought a washing machine. Perhaps it was a reward for Daisy's faithfulness and willingness to put aside her own dreams for her sake. The laundry which had required soaking all night and rubbing on a board all the next day could now be done in half a day. Without doubt, the difficult task of doing that laundry by hand in pre-washing-machine days helped to develop the grit and determination to stick to a job until it was done — 133 pieces this week, 69 pieces the following week, or 158 pieces the next. It did indeed help to "make a lady" of her.

The fall and early winter months passed and the Bubys decided that the time had come for Daisy to return to Pasadena. Patience, prayer, and hard work were rewarded at last, and preparations were made for her to enroll in Pilgrim Academy for the second semester. It was February 1921. The long delay was over, and Daisy joyfully went back where she knew she was supposed to be.

Chapter 3

Letting God Lead

Mexico, Not India

This is what the Lord says — your Redeemer, the Holy One of Israel: "I am the Lord your God, who teaches you what is best for you, who directs you in the way you should go" (Isaiah 48:17 NIV).

*T*he front steps of the dormitory at Pilgrim Bible College in Pasadena were the scene of much laughter, hugging, and squeals of delight as Daisy's friends rushed out to meet her. When she finally emerged from the tangle of loving arms, she could not keep back the tears of joy. It was as if she had never been away. Everyone helped to carry her baggage inside, but it wasn't to stay there long.

God answered her prayer for work almost immediately by opening a Christian home where she earned room and board and a few dollars a week. The sympathetic older couple treated her like a daughter.

Daisy's schedule of classes included required courses toward a high school diploma along with Spanish I and II and some Bible courses. In addition, she took another practical nursing class in Pasadena.

The early part of that semester was a time of spiritual soul-searching for Daisy. She wondered how she could long to be in every service and be reluctant to go all at the same time. Even though there were so many "definite" answers to prayer, as she would put it, her mind was troubled about her own standing with the Lord. She wrote, "Everything is in a muddle." Three days later she said, "Got my mind straightened out. Chapel services an inspiration and test, too."

She dreaded to go to chapel fearing that she would have to go to the altar, but she desperately wanted peace and assurance.

25

A great deal of "close" preaching and her own sensitive con-science kept her in turmoil for weeks. She even missed classes and meals trying, all alone, to come to terms with her reluctance to admit that time and circumstances had shaken her commit-ment to her Lord. She finally faced the fact that there was still a great deal of pride at the root of her problems. The competent, controlled Buby image had to be replaced with the vulnerability of admitting that she was human like everyone else!

It wasn't so difficult to talk about her own personal battle after she saw Francisco's sister, Leonor Soltero, struggle with her call and commitment to the Lord. That problem was settled at the chapel altar one day, and Daisy reported that Leonor got so happy she cried.

By the end of February, Daisy was able to testify about her-self with certainty and peace once again, "I believe more than ever that the Lord's will for me is the mission field."

At the end of that school year, Leonor Soltero went home with Daisy to San Diego. She spent several weeks at the Buby home that summer before joining the Solteros in Mexico. Mama Buby and Daisy helped her prepare clothing and supplies for her life on the mission field. The Bubys took this Mexican-American girl to their hearts as if she were another daughter and cherished sister. At last, the time came for her to leave, and with great excitement, her "family" and friends sent her off to her shining adventure.

The following year passed quickly, filled with school, nurs-ing, and substitute teaching. It was a year of repeated spiritual crises for Daisy as the demands of heavy schedules took their toll on body and spirit. She weathered the storm through the Spirit-led counseling of G. Arnold Hodgin, the brother-in-law of Seth Rees, who had become president of the school. She learned the valuable lesson that year of distinguishing between fluctuating emotions, physical weariness, and spiritual failure. She wrote in her diary, "Bro. and Sis. Hodgin will never know how much they have meant to me. They have encouraged and helped me through."

All that year, Daisy was reminded of Mexico again and again in chapels and in letters from Leonor. Daisy fairly danced for joy when one of those letters announced Leonor's marriage to Salvador Ponce, the first graduate from the Mexican Bible School. The Bubys responded with gifts for the bride and money to help in setting up their home in the mountains where they were to start a new church. Months later another letter announced the anticipation of their first baby, and Mama Buby went into action again to provide all that was needed for her missionary "daughter" in the mountains of Mexico.

Daisy's final year at Pasadena Bible Training College passed in a whirl of study, work, and spiritual growth. At the end of January she wrote, "A month of new experiences in grace. I didn't know that Christianity meant so much."

Senior sneak day came early in March, but it would forever be recorded in Daisy's memory for another reason. An inconceivable message from Mexico was waiting for her when she arrived back at school. Leonor died in childbirth at their remote mountain church in Mexico!

It was a terrible shock! It could not be! Leonor was dead, and she was there such a short time, not even two years! She and Salvador Ponce went to their mountain home to pastor after their marriage. Less than a year later, she died three days after giving birth to their first child, because there was no medical help. And the baby was stillborn. Poor Salvador was devastated, and the mountain people who loved her so much mourned inconsolably.

Tears rolled down Daisy's face as she tried to picture her vibrantly alive friend, Leonor, dead! It seemed so senseless. An overwhelming conviction began to grip her mind and heart. If only she had been there, this might not have happened. She must not let another year pass without getting on with her preparation to be a missionary nurse. She knew with the certainty of divine conviction that her mission field was to be Mexico, not India.

She announced her new revelation to Seth Rees as she sat in the Rees home, copying the letter bearing the sad news to send to her mother. She explained that his strong emphasis on missions had contributed to her resolve to be a missionary, and now she knew where.

His blunt reply stunned her momentarily. "But Daisy, I didn't mean you!"

"Why did he say that?" she questioned silently. "Is it because he doesn't have confidence in me? No. He has trusted me with responsibilities in the church and school. Is it because he thinks I don't possess the qualities a missionary should have? Maybe. Is it because he thinks they need me here at home? Probably, because they call me every time anyone in the Rees family is ill. But there are others who can take care of the sick here. Surely he understands that if I'm called, I must obey."

With that same radiant Daisy smile hiding that same Daisy stubbornness, she declared, "God will have to make me into a missionary." Her mind was clear and her decision was firm. She would become a missionary nurse as soon as possible!

Daisy graduated from high school in 1923 and went home to San Diego, waiting to know from the Lord how and when nurses training would begin. She luxuriated in the certainty of her call and the sense of God's approval on her life as she pictured herself in nurses uniform and cap. And the scene of her service was to be Mexico instead of India.

Chapter 4

Courage To Overcome
By Faith!

And my God will meet all your needs according to his glorious riches in Christ Jesus (Philippians 4:19 NIV).

Nursing school at last! Daisy enrolled at Huntington Memorial School of Nursing in Pasadena on February 4, 1924, with financial help from her parents, and by saving every penny she could from various nursing jobs. On the day of her arrival, she was taken into the loving care of a former missionary nurse who helped her get her uniforms ready, and prepared her mentally for the rigorous tasks ahead.

Hard work and study filled the days and nights to overflowing. Entries in her diary during the training years were short and revealing.

> *February 4, 1924. Date of entrance in nursing school. Sewed on uniform in Jean Pound's room, unpacked, had uniform inspection.*

> *February 16, 1924. Enjoying nursing classes.*

> *November 5, 1924. New home for the Buby family!*

> *November 29, 1924. Alvin and Violet's wedding Day.*

> *January 6, 1925. I just love my work and can hardly wait from one day to another to see how my patients have gotten along.*

> *June 7, 1925. Solteros at church — talked with her about electives, and she said maternity.*

January 1, 1926. On duty this a.m. At 11:15 ambulances began rushing in. I helped put injured to bed. A large stand fell during the Rose Bowl Parade and many injured came here. Looks like 100's. It is awful! I worked in Op. Rm. 'til 8:30 p.m. So tired. No half days for us.

January 3, 1926. Worked straight 8 hours and went to Y.P. and church in the evening. Kilbournes spoke in missionary service. They are splendid.

June 4, 1926. Letter from Sis. Soltero said, "I love you, Daisy, and I'm sure we're going to get along fine together."

August 3, 1926. Filled out application blank to the missionary board.

October 31, 1926. Went to see Nella and Ethel True. Told me a great deal about San Luis in Mexico.

February 20, 1927. Finished training today noon after a busy morning in the lab. Am sorry to leave this home of mine. I love it all so much.

May 5, 1927. Graduation Day! Home to San Diego.

May 26, 1927. Prayed and started a letter to Mrs. Soltero.

In that letter Daisy told of her graduation and her intention to come to Mexico as soon as possible. Nettie Soltero's jubilant congratulatory response encouraged and perplexed her.

My dear Daisy,

I was so glad to get your little letter and to know that at last you have graduated.

Congratulations! I know it meant everything to stay among ungodly nurses and doctors such a long time, but at last you are out.

I am so glad you are still planning to come to Mexico, for we do need you so much among the Indians. I will proceed to answer your questions. For traveling mule back you will need a good khaki suit. We prefer the riding skirts here as the habit of ladies wearing trousers has not become general.

*You will need boots or good heavy shoes with leggins. You
should have a raincoat for walking out from house to house,
and bring a rain-proof hat.*

*A good mule costs from $75 to $100, but we have
bought several fairly good ones for $50. One can get a good
burro for $20. Bring your folding cot, your bedding, pillows,
sheets, tablecloths, napkins and plenty of clothes for yourself. We use cow's milk, and it costs 10 cents a quart.*

*Learn to be a warrior in prayer and faith, for you will
have need of those weapons here.*

Yours in Jesus,
Nettie W. Soltero

Daisy pondered the letter from Nettie Soltero. She had
thought she was prepared for the challenge to which she had
committed herself. But was she?

"Mules cost up to $100! Does that mean I will have to buy
my own mule? And I am to ride a mule?! And why did she
mention the burro? O, Lord, help! I don't even know how to
ride a horse, let alone a mule."

The girl who lived in a beautiful suburban home built by a
master carpenter for his beloved family suddenly began to face
the realities of pioneer mountain missionary work. The last sentence of the letter was heeded on the spot. She had been doing
a lot of praying already, but it seemed more necessary than ever
now. Once again, natural shyness and gentleness struggled
against the dawning realization of just how rugged her life
might be.

It had taken huge amounts of grit and determination to keep
plodding on in nursing school, but the goal of becoming a missionary nurse and the encouragement given by family and spiritual mentors had pulled her through.

Now, how was she to get enough money together to buy all
she needed, including that mule? There was no promise of support from anywhere. The Pilgrim Holiness Church with Seth
Rees now as its leader had turned down her application because
of lack of funds, but gave their blessing if she could go on her
own. Times were hard and lack of money was squeezing bud-
gets down to the bare necessities, even in the church.

Far ahead of mules on Daisy's list of priorities was the hospital she had designed with the help of her father. It was only a
dream on paper, but she often visualized herself in the simple
building delivering babies, ministering to the sick, and caring for

the wounded. Her father promised to come to Mexico to help make the dream a reality.

She would have to pray in her supplies and support, or work for them, and so Daisy resigned herself to wait a while longer for Mexico. Six months later, encouragement came again from Nettie.

> *We are so glad that God is making your call stronger each day, and we know that where there is a will there's a way, especially when it is God's will. We know you are badly needed in Mexico, and we believe there will be a way.*
>
> *Francisco and I have talked over it and prayed over it, and we do want you so badly. We feel sure there must be some way. Francisco says for you to go on saving for fare. Buy plenty of clothes to last you two or three years, and provide yourself with bedding.*
>
> *As to coming married (an older missionary friend had advised this alternative), naturally you could do very little as a trained nurse if you were tied up with a home. I know you pretty well. I do not take you to be very "soft" or "silly," and do not believe you would be falling in love with all the native workers the first year on the field.*

Daisy mused, "Thank goodness, they trust me to behave myself. And I will." Her mind wandered back over the years to the young men who had shown interest in her, not one of whom was called to be a missionary. At one point she had even asked God to give her and Mexico a doctor, but with a twinge of sadness she realized that it probably was not going to happen.

Her thoughts lingered on the last time she had dealt with the issue of marriage. After nursing school was finished, and she came home to work and wait to go to Mexico, another charming young man captured her attention. Several weeks later, she prepared for an expected Sunday morning rendezvous with special care. She decided to wear her flowing white, lace-trimmed graduation dress and white shoes. Her wavy light brown hair was attractively arranged, and the anticipation of the meeting made her blue eyes sparkle and her naturally pink cheeks glow.

When he did not even come to church that Sunday, her dream was shattered. Most of Sunday afternoon was spent sobbing out her bitter disappointment to her Lord in the quietness of her room. She remembered her prayer of long ago that God would not allow anyone to cause her to deviate from His plan. The dream of marriage was surrendered that day into the hands of her loving Heavenly Father.

Yes, the Solteros were right. She was determined not to be "soft" or "silly." The long road to Mexico had cost too much for her to allow romantic dreams to destroy the fulfillment of God's plan for her life.

Several more weeks passed by, and Daisy became desperate to get to Mexico. The church in Pasadena with William Neff replacing Seth Rees as pastor gave their approval, but promised no support. She finally wrote to tell the Solteros that she was willing to come by faith!

Nettie responded confidently, "We are glad you are beginning to look at San Luis as your home church. That sounds good to me, sounds like you mean business, and we assure you we are going to do all in our power to bring you. Don't forget to pray mightily, for God is on the throne, and He can send you even if the board can't."

The final GO signal came in a letter from Nettie dated March 15, 1928.

Dear Daisy,

We want to make you a new offer. Our people are very anxious to have you come, and we are going to offer you room and board free. The only thing we cannot offer you is a salary at present, but feel sure that God will provide it in time. Do you still think you can come in June? Just save up enough to pay your fare and have a little money when you get here, and come by faith.

You need not fear to come. It is not as if you were going out to a strange country without knowing anybody. You are just coming to your other home, that is all. We have an extra room pretty well furnished by the church, and you can occupy that while you are with us here in San Luis, and when we send you out over the district, there will always be a place for you in the pastors' homes.

With much love,
Nettie W. de Soltero

Daisy was ecstatic. "As I prayed about it, God gave me Joshua 1:9, 'Have not I commanded thee? Be strong and of a good courage; be not afraid, neither be thou dismayed; for the Lord thy God is with thee whithersoever thou goest.' With that promise of His care wherever I went, I knew that I must go."

Daisy made her reservations to leave for Mexico by rail on July 17, 1928, at 9:05 a.m.!

Now the letters flew back and forth between Mexico and San Diego. Nettie Soltero, always full of irrepressible enthusiasm, answered Daisy's acceptance letter.

> *Dear Daisy,*
>
> *I received your letter where you tell me that you are really coming, and I was so happy that I jumped and clapped my hands together. The girls laughed at me, but I could hardly contain myself. How wonderful! I am so glad that God is helping you so much. I knew he would if he wanted you to come, and that is proof positive. Everybody here is so happy because you are coming. Tell your dear mother that bugs and snakes are about as plentiful here in San Luis as they are in San Diego!*

Daisy was propelled through final preparations by more encouragement from Nettie in April 1928, a letter which also included a long list of things to bring along. She went to work with a vengeance, buying some items with her own funds and asking the women's organization for help with others. Packing according to instructions was a tedious chore, especially when different instructions came from different sources. In characteristic Daisy fashion, she repeated the process four times in order to make it perfect. Finally, everything was ready. It was the first time to pack for the mission field, but it would not be the last.

Part II

Missionary Orientation Years

Getting Into The Saddle

"Thy part is to yield thyself, His part is to work; and never, never will He give thee any command which is not accompanied by ample power to obey it."

Hannah Whitall Smith

Chapter 5

The Call Fulfilled

Mexico at Last

The Lord himself goes before you and will be with you;
he will never leave you nor forsake you. Do not be afraid;
do not be discouraged (Deuteronomy 31:8 NIV).

*D*aisy sat at a writing table in the hospital, eyes brimming with tears as she read over the letter she had written to her parents. She was scheduled to leave for Mexico in six days! Her last few days of private duty were excruciatingly difficult, a severe test of her resolve to be a missionary nurse. After preparing her very ill and very ill-tempered patient for the night, she slipped into a vacant room to cry her heart out to God.

She was suffering from a severe case of homesickness, even more terrible than any she had experienced while away from her family during her school years. God allowed her to return home to work for a while before going to Mexico, and now it seemed that she couldn't tear herself away!

> *San Diego*
> *July 11, 1928*
> *Mercy Hospital*

Dearest Mama and Papa,

Since I don't know how to express my love or apprecia-tion in plain audible English words, I hope you both under-stand my unexpressed feelings anyway. I sure do thank you for your help in every way, in your cooperation with me and my plans, your Christian influence, your prayers, your financial support when you are so hard pressed, and your help in giving time to my preparations. I won't forget it, and I have prayed God's richest blessings may be upon you.

I am glad that I've been able to pay some of the money you have spent for me during my school days back to you in this past year. Only wish it could have been more. However, I feel clear about leaving you and your financial difficulties to God, while I go to try to help poor lost Mexicans. If only I can be a blessing to them! I feel so terribly unworthy, tonight, of ever having a call to missionary work. I hope and pray that I may be a real one. A large share of my success as a missionary will be due to your training and prayer, and the other part to the prayers of my many wonderful friends.

Do not worry about me down in Mexico. I shall take care of myself as best I can. With a conscience void of offense toward God or man, and God's love and peace in my heart, it doesn't matter what may happen to the body. I will take care of myself, though, for the sake of the ones who will need me in these coming weeks and months.

> *With lots of love,*
> *Daisy*

Writing that letter helped ease the hurt of leaving Mama and Papa, and God did the rest. Three days before departure, all homesickness left her, and by her own testimony, never returned whether she was near them or so far away for so long that home seemed like an unreal dream.

Daisy's do-or-die mentality, her courage, and her cheerful optimism pulled her through scores of adventures into the unknown. It began with the trip to Mexico.

The journey was scheduled for July 17, 1928, long before anyone could have foretold the historic events which were to happen in Mexico that day. All preparations were made according to instructions from Mrs. Soltero, and armed with her promise from the Lord, Daisy boarded the train in San Diego. As loved ones on the platform waved good-bye, Daisy waved back and settled into her seat on the train. She was delightfully happy and completely at rest in the conviction that at last, she was going to the place of her calling. The only difficulty was the extreme heat.

July 17. Up early. "Daddy Mays" took my trunk to the depot. Sis. Chapman was with us at the breakfast table. Mama, Papa, Billie, and others came to see me off. Took

> *the 9:05 train. . . . A lovely trip until noon, then hot and hotter, 113 degrees in the valley. At Yuma I changed cars on the same train. Went to bed at 8:30 very tired and hot. Not many traveling.*

During the second day of travel, the passengers, including Daisy, were stunned with the news that President Obregon of Mexico had been assassinated the day before. It might have been enough to cause the faint of heart to turn back, but not Daisy. She clung to the promise God gave her, "Have not I commanded thee? Be strong and of a good courage; be not afraid, neither be thou dismayed: for the Lord thy God is with thee whithersoever thou goest" Joshua 1:9.

Daisy's natural curiosity, her happy smile and gentle friendliness made it easy to chat with fellow passengers. Two of the conductors stopped to visit and learn where she was going and why. She must have looked like the quiet, dedicated young woman that she was, five feet three inches tall and in robust good health. Tiny curls escaped from the soft bun at the nape of her neck and peeped out from under her brimmed hat. They made a pleasing frame for her happy round face. Her clothing, made by her own hands, was sturdy and simple, but attractive and neat.

Her ever-present diary recorded the journey in great detail. The assassination of Mexico's president rated only one sentence, however.

> *July 18. President Obregon of Mexico assassinated yesterday. Joshua 1:9. A cool comfortable night and plenty of sleep. The day was very pleasant through Texas — cactus and dry dusty hills and plains. Some cattle, adobe huts, and Mexicans. El Paso is a little town on the muddy Rio Grande. A few farms scattered, but so much unused land. The conductor sat and talked to me for a while. To bed early.*

Not knowing what to expect on the other side of the border, Daisy transferred from one station to another in San Antonio, Texas, and settled her belongings in the train for the last portion of her journey. Most of her traveling companions were Mexicans returning home. Sounds of Spanish filled the air as they deposited their numerous baskets and bundles under the seats and at their feet. She became keenly aware that she was among people whose language and culture she did not know. If they were bothered by the death of their president, she could not detect it. She experienced no fear, only overwhelming love and a determination to learn to communicate. Her radiant smile and kind ways soon won friends for the journey.

> *July 19. Joshua 1:9. Arrived in San Antonio at 3:35 a.m. Our car switched and transferred to the other train depot. Train left at 9:45 a.m. I rode in the open coach with the poor Mexicans. Such an awful dusty trip to Laredo. Gave the lead dog (gift to Daisy) to a Mexican baby to play with on the way. Arrived safely at Laredo, rechecked my trunk, went through immigration office OK and customs. No duty but $11.00 head tax. Left Laredo, Mexico, at 6:45, and saw a beautiful sunset. Desert.*

After the ordeal of immigration and customs in Laredo, Mexico, Daisy began to realize that she was actually in the land of her calling. As the train left the station and slowly gained speed, she turned toward the window, eagerly watching the passing scenes of her adopted homeland. A beautiful sunset cast a golden glow over the stark poverty on every side. Long after darkness obscured the outside world, her head whirled with the sights and sounds of the last few hours. Sleep finally came with the words of Matthew 11:5 going over and over in her mind accompanied by the sound of the train wheels on the track, ". . . and the poor have the gospel preached to them . . . and the poor have the gospel preached to them . . . and the poor have the gospel preached to them."

The night hours passed, and the morning light of her last day of travel revealed desert dotted with cactus and pulque plants, small towns of adobe houses, cities with narrow dusty streets, and finally the tree-clad mountains of north central Mexico. Always there were people walking, riding horses or burros, children playing, and women carrying loads on their heads or washing clothes in small streams. The drab brown of the earth was accented by tropical green foliage and the brilliant rainbow colors of Mexican ponchos (capes) worn by the people. Daisy's heart began to pound with anticipation as she realized they were approaching journey's end.

And then, San Luis Potosi at last! The train pulled into the station late in the afternoon of July 20. The welcoming group on the platform included Francisco and Nettie Soltero, students, and workers. She was "home" at last!

At the welcoming service that evening, Daisy listened to several glowing speeches interpreted by Mrs. Soltero. When it came time for her to respond, she decided to try some of her Spanish learned in high school ten years before. She said rather timidly, "Good morning, my brothers," and it was evening! It was several months before she learned of her mistake, because no one even dared to smile lest they discourage her.

The first order of business for Daisy after unpacking her things and getting settled into her room was to explore her new home and to become acquainted with the new people in her life. Somewhere in the back of her mind, she had known all along she would have to learn Spanish, but it did not take long for her to realize that it was an absolute essential. She made a vow to learn as fast as possible. Nettie Soltero became her teacher along with Virginia, the lovely young Mexican senorita assigned to be her companion and helper.

She described her language-learning struggle. "Language study was slow, but there was no other way if I wanted to know what was being said. All conversation was in Spanish. There is a saying in Spanish, 'by reason or by force,' and that is how it was with me.

"My first prayer in Spanish was really by force. When the other missionaries and I had prayer together, they each prayed in Spanish. Oh, how I had hoped that someone would pray in English! I had been in Mexico four long months, and there was no reason why I shouldn't be able to pray in Spanish, so I began, 'Padre Celestial.' My head felt inflated and my brains shrank to the size of a small walnut running around inside! I held my head to try to steady my brains, prayed one sentence and said, 'Amen.' I thought that I would never be able to pray from the heart in that language, but the time came when I preferred to pray in Spanish."

Eventually she learned to preach, teach, and converse in Spanish so well that the Mexicans said she sounded like them. Daisy learned to read her Spanish Bible, and often turned to it to study scriptures that seemed obscure in English. That proficiency was not achieved, however, until after many months and some prodding by Francisco Soltero's comments, "That was good, Daisy, but not yet Mexican!"

Chapter 6

Fitting Into A New Culture

Becoming Mexican

Though I am free and belong to no man, I make myself a slave to everyone, to win as many as possible . . . I have become all things to all men so that by all possible means I might save some. I do all this for the sake of the gospel, that I may share in its blessings (I Corinthians 9:19, 22-23 NIV).

*F*or months before Daisy's arrival, the growing "family" at the Soltero mission home had prayed for a more spacious place, especially now that they expected a new missionary. Miraculously, God made a lovely old Spanish style stone and stucco mansion on a small acreage available to them for an incredibly low price. Daisy arrived in San Luis just in time to enjoy the excitement of answered prayer, and to learn another lesson in "living by faith." Besides enough room for everyone, there were several acres of land to accommodate a few farm animals and extensive gardens in addition to a field of alfalfa.

San Luis, Potosi, Mex.
August 5, 1928

Dear Mama,

We moved into our new home yesterday a.m.. We only had to move about a block so the boys carried everything over — including the piano and Bro. Soltero's rolltop desk. We had almost everything over by noon, and quite straightened up by evening. Only the chickens and the chicken houses are left.

Our home here includes 12 rooms, bath (with bathtub and toilet), storeroom, one hall and two large patios. At present I am with the girls in a bedroom 15 1/2 by 23 feet. Our floor is red brick tile and is even with the ground. From one door we have a beautiful view of the hills.

There is one bedroom that needs to be remodeled that is just off of Bro. Soltero's study. That will be their bedroom, and I will have the room they now occupy for myself.

Mr. and Mrs. Sanchez (Mexican student/pastor) who occupy 3 rooms in the other house are to have a small 3-room house here on the property as soon as it is made ready for them.

Daisy became "Mamacita" (Mommie) to nine girls ranging in age from seven to nineteen. Solteros were responsible for seven boys. All the young people were sent by their parents in the mountain churches to study in the city. Francisco and Nettie, who had no children of their own, joyfully received the young people. Several of the boys who felt called to preach attended public school during the day and Bible school classes in the evening.

The new house soon became a beehive of activity as the members of the big family performed the tasks assigned to them. Solteros believed that in order to produce successful pastors, they should teach everyone to study as hard as they could and work as hard as they could. Each of their "children" must learn to love God and His work with all their hearts in a caring, sharing family atmosphere. Besides that, everyone who wanted to be a pastor must learn to trust God to supply all his needs.

Nettie and Francisco modeled all those concepts before their family consistently, day in and day out. No one worked harder or gave more of themselves to the work than they. Daisy was to learn even more about the dynamics of prayer and faith that were at the heart of the powerful and fruitful ministry of Francisco and Nettie Soltero.

Daisy's hours were filled with studying Spanish, looking after the girls, and doing numerous tasks that seemed more like mothering than being a missionary. She cheerfully spent her own money for cloth with which to make dresses for her girls. Hours were spent coaching them in their lessons and teaching them how to do their chores. It was when she was putting her nursing skills to work that she felt more like she was doing the missionary work God had called her to do.

> *I have quite a clinic here now. Bro. Soltero and Jose with sore eyes, Jose Francisco (Indian) with sprained wrist and finger, Seraphin with a sprained finger and a canker sore in his mouth, 2 boys with ring worm, 2 girls with scalp trouble — I don't know what to call it. Bro. Mascorro with a sore finger. Besides these who have not been discharged as cured, are 2 with slivers, 3 with stomach upsets, 2 with colds and 1 with headache. And a number of chickens with chicken pox, and a setting hen (no eggs) with chicken fleas.*
>
> *It is my duty, also, to keep the deer well by feeding her a cup of bran and milk each morning.*

If Daisy ever suffered culture shock, no one knew it, not even she! She was too busy to be lonely, and too enthralled with her new surroundings to be bored. Solteros saw to it that her needs were met and that there were special treats along the way.

> *I haven't taken the last Kodak picture yet. I must do it soon. Have so much to do, and am not fully organized yet, so I really waste some time every day. There is so much to see and get used to.*
>
> *I've had ice cream in town with Bro. and Sis. Soltero 5 times already. They call me their little sister. They are certainly fine to live with. They are so good to me. They are so sensible about everything.*
>
> *They got me some lovely new furniture, a white iron bed, springs and mattress, dresser, wash stand (with pretty enamel basin, pitcher, 2 soap dishes with covers, slop jar and chamber), a rocking chair and a beautiful desk.*
>
> *Anyone is safe in San Luis with a large bag of silver on his shoulder. They carry their silver in large bags of 1,000 pesos each in an open truck with only 2 men, unarmed, to take it to the banks. You can't do that in California many times. I enjoy freedom here. I really believe that any girl alone here in Mexico is much safer than in the States. It feels that way!*
>
> *Don't worry about my going out alone. I feel very safe, but Solteros are careful that I always have someone along.*

Relationships in the big house were warm and easy. Daisy responded to the fun and laughter with rather uncharacteristic behavior at times. But who could resist when it was Francisco Soltero himself who was the biggest tease of all?

Bro. Soltero was acting up Saturday evening in the kitchen, and I took Sis. Soltero's part against him. I felt it my duty to throw a half glass of water into his face. When I hid behind Sis. Soltero, he came and poured a quarter glass of water down my back. Oh, but it was cold! Then he ran and locked himself in his study.

During the first several weeks, Daisy suffered with a severe stomach upset which she concluded was due to the peppery hot Mexican food. On one of those days when she could not eat the customary brown beans and chili, Francisco came home from town with a gift for her. "Here is some fresh bread and butter for you, little sister. I don't think Nettie is feeding you right."

"How thoughtful, but please don't worry about me," responded Daisy, somewhat embarrassed that she had not been able to quickly adjust to Mexican food. "As soon as my system becomes accustomed to this spicy hot food, I'll be fine."

Learning to eat Mexican food was just one more step in making Mexico her home, or to put it Francisco's way, "becoming Mexican."

Another Soltero strategy to help Daisy become Mexican, was to involve her in the local church in San Luis. Letters written home during those first months tell of singing solos in Spanish, participating in the youth choir, even directing the youth meetings through an interpreter. She found visiting the homes of the members with the deaconess a deeply satisfying experience. Before long she was accepted as one of them as she entered into their sorrows and joys. She felt more and more at home with each passing day.

In fact, she felt comfortable enough with her newfound Mexican family to write a rather startling letter to her parents.

*Don't be **too** shocked if I should marry a Mexican, for if I **should** find one I liked as well as I do Virginia, and he asked me, I am sure I wouldn't hesitate in accepting. If you could meet some of my **nice** Mexicans here in San Luis, you wouldn't mind much. However, no one has asked me, and moreover I've not met the free Mexican whom I'd care to marry, so there is yet **great possibility** that I remain a spinster the rest of my days.*

She was annoyed by a letter from a young man back in San Diego whom she did not admire. Daisy, who was usually so proper and thoughtful, chose not to answer the letter, but asked her mother to convey a message for her.

At your convenience (don't rush yourself), please tell that fellow that I received the 13 songs, and that Bro. and Sis Solter were pleased to get them. (Oh, not too pleased, just a little.) If he should happen to ask you, he is not going to receive an answer from me! I am too busy writing my real friends to be bothered with him.

The persistent young man wrote a letter to Francisco Soltero a few weeks later, proposing to come to San Luis to take charge of their Bible school. Daisy saw through the strategy at once and announced to the Solteros, "If that young man comes here, I shall escape to the mountains before he arrives."

Francisco's quick reply was, "I am sure he will follow you there."

In consternation, Daisy begged them not to let him come. Neither Nettie nor Francisco was impressed with his abilities or humility, and so Francisco wrote a letter which put an end to the whole idea.

Daisy settled back into her duties with a quiet heart, waiting for the day when she really would go to the mountains to be a missionary nurse. In the meantime, she learned to ride a horse in preparation for that day. She was thrilled when Solteros asked her to teach classes in health and hygiene to their "family" and at the workers' institute which was held three months after she arrived in Mexico.

In addition to caring for her girls and teaching those classes with Nettie's help as interpreter, she was kept busy ministering to an almost endless stream of sick folks. Even Francisco learned that this missionary nurse was not one to play games when it came to her primary ministry.

Last night I doctored Bro. Soltero by force. He has a bad cold in his head and throat and refused the medicine of Sis. Soltero. So I just came along with mine and made him take it. He said afterwards that I wasn't afraid of anyone. Just came a few minutes ago to ask if I didn't have mail to send and that Juan and Salvador wanted to treat him to ice cream if that would be all right. I told them to give him at least 2 dishes!

Those first months in Mexico included a trip to a mountain village where one of their student pastors was planting a church. The sights and sounds, the extreme poverty of the people, and their hunger for the gospel were riveted on her mind for all time. She even took the difficult bus trip over cobblestone roads

in stride. The visit to the small mining town served to deepen
her growing love for Mexico and its people. She wrote about her
experience to a Women's Missionary Society back in San Diego.

> *San Pedro is a very old gold and silver mining town.*
> *They have mined there over 300 years. The houses, built*
> *along the mountain canyon, are adobe or rock, and built on*
> *the steep hillsides. Many people have dug a room or two out*
> *of the side of the mountain and have poles or rocks for a*
> *front wall. Their door is window and stove pipe as well.*
> *Their floor is of rocks and dirt. They live very simply.*
>
> *The two-room house where Virginia (my companion)*
> *and I were entertained belongs to Brother and Sister*
> *Rodriguez, the layman who started the church. This man*
> *and his wife gave us their only beds, one iron bed and a*
> *homemade cot, and they slept on the floor. Brother Soltero*
> *and Sanchez, the student pastor, slept in another home.*
>
> *The little church is a 2-room house. Bro. Soltero plans*
> *to take out the wall between the 2 rooms and enlarge front-*
> *wards to make a seating capacity for 100.*
>
> *The first evening we had 28 besides the four of us, each*
> *family carrying a carbon mine lantern. I played the little*
> *organ and everyone sang as hard as he could. Brother*
> *Soltero preached, and when he asked those who were not*
> *satisfied in their hearts and wanted to be Christians to come*
> *forward and kneel at the little altar, 5 women responded at*
> *once, and almost everyone else held up his hand for prayer.*

After that visit to San Pedro, Daisy could hardly wait for the
trip to the Huasteca, the mountain area surrounding Valles
which was fast becoming the most important part of all the
work. The trip had been scheduled and re-scheduled almost
from the time of her arrival. This was the area from which most
of the ·young people in their "family" came, the place where
Daisy was to be permanently stationed. It was the place of her
dreams ever since Leonor had died there.

> *When I live in Temalacaco (in the Huesteca) I'll have*
> *clinics in the little towns around and go back and forth by*
> *horseback. Won't that be interesting? Virginia is planning*
> *on studying midwifery here in San Luis, but she will proba-*
> *bly help me in the mountains after she has finished.*
>
> *I showed Virginia the plans for my clinic and hospital.*
> *Drew the sketch in the dust for her.*

Daisy took the precious drawings of the hospital out of their hiding place and looked at them longingly when she could no longer endure the waiting. Would she ever be able to go? Would the dream ever become reality? Was this really God's plan for her life? If so, she was convinced He would provide the funds and direct the Solteros.

But first things first. The time for the first and major payment on their new property loomed like a specter on the horizon, and the promised funds had not yet come. Many hours were spent in fasting and prayer claiming the promises, and God answered dramatically. The money came from headquarters just in time, and a thanksgiving fiesta was the order of the day.

Our school is assured, but not my clinic at present.

Bro. Soltero says I'm one of the family, and I'm to share everything from a banana to a fortune with trials and lack of money included.

Finances were tight at headquarters, so Daisy was still not "on contract" with the denomination even though they approved her as one of their missionaries. The money for her support came from friends little by little in answer to prayer, $5.00 one time, $2.00 another. Once in a while someone sent $20.00. Daisy kept personal needs to a minimum in order to give toward the needs of the work. There never seemed to be enough funds for all the demands, let alone to build a hospital. Delays and changes in plans for the visit to the beloved Huasteca made the dream seem even more remote.

Dear Mama,

Bro. Soltero's plans have been changed. Guess we won't get to the Huasteca until December now. By that time I hope Paul and Anna (Grout) will be here, and they will go with us.

The Grouts arrived before December, and at last the promised trip was scheduled for November 28. Mrs. Soltero volunteered to stay at home in San Luis so the rest could make the journey. Lest anyone think she was being heroic to stay behind, she quickly assured everyone that she did not particularly enjoy riding mules or horses, and that she was better equipped to be mother and teacher to the young people at home than to cope with rugged mountain life.

With great anticipation, Daisy packed her medicines, her bedding, and her clothing including sturdy riding skirts, rain gear, and riding boots. She was ready for another excursion into the unknown. She could now tolerate fiery hot Mexican food, and make herself understood in Spanish with a limited vocabulary. She thoroughly enjoyed life where God had put her. After being in San Luis for four and a half months, she was enough Mexican to be introduced to her future home in the mountains.

Chapter 7

Anticipation Becomes Reality

Off to the Huasteca

Then I came to them of the captivity at Telabib, that dwelt by the river of Chebar, and I sat where they sat, and remained there astonished among them seven days (Ezekiel 3:15 KJV).

Thursday morning, November 28, was the day Daisy had been looking forward to long before her arrival in San Luis. Anticipation made her eyes dance with the innocent wonder of a child waiting for Christmas.

Francisco Soltero, Paul and Anna Grout, and Daisy boarded the morning train in San Luis bound for Valles, the small city in the southeastern corner of their state from which the surrounding mountain towns could be reached. It was the area known as the Huasteca.

They stowed their baggage under and over their second class, low-backed wooden seats and tried to make themselves comfortable. Once again, Daisy eagerly watched the passing countryside of her adopted home as the train moved southward.

The first five hours after leaving San Luis were like southern California with bare mountains, cactus, and bush-covered plains. Then they came into lush mountains covered with tropical trees, vines, tree ferns, moss, and palms. Abundant rains fed dancing mountain streams which plunged down canyons and over fern-fringed falls. Tropical flowers brightened the blanket of green which covered the rocky mountainsides — brilliant red poinsettias, hibiscus, and tiny pink blossoms on thick vines. Wild orchids clung to the trunks of the trees.

Daisy and the Grouts thought they were entering a tropical botanical paradise. Francisco Soltero, the pioneer of this mountain work, knew that they would have to fight their way through that thick foliage and across the swollen rivers on horseback to reach their destinations in the mountains. During the last hour and a half of their trip, the train descended several thousand feet down the mountains into the natural bowl where Valles (pronounced Vah-yeahs, meaning valleys) was located. The brakes on the train were smoking when they arrived at the bottom.

At the end of nine and a half uncomfortable hours, it was wonderful to be met at the station by members of the small congregation in Valles, given their meal, and put to bed. The next morning, they discovered that the road over which they were to go by auto for the first part of their journey was impassible because of the rains. They waited two days for horses to be brought all the way to Valles by two Aztec Indian men. The time was spent encouraging the believers who had no church building and were hungry for spiritual food and fellowship. Brother Soltero was looking forward to organizing a church in this strategic city.

It was a strange looking caravan which finally started on the journey toward the mountains. Three horses and a mule carried the Mexican superintendent and the three new missionaries. Two mules loaded with their suitcases, bedding rolls, and boxes of medicines were led by two Indians on foot. Francisco Soltero and Paul Grout rode their horses confidently, but Anna, who had never ridden before, was nervous and a little afraid.

Daisy rode her steed with uneasy grace. With a wry smile, she remembered her dismay of many months before when Nettie Soltero's letter had hinted that she might be riding a mule. A horse would have been fine, but here she was on a little black mule for the very first time in her life, hanging onto the saddle horn for dear life with one hand. With the other, she tried to keep her riding skirt from being caught on the bushes which reached out from the mountainsides as they rode along slippery, muddy trails. There was no need to guide her animal with the reins, because he knew the way very well and had a mind of his own.

She blamed Francisco's strange sense of humor for hiring the mule for her. But after the first few anxious miles, she relaxed and enjoyed the rhythmic movement of her surefooted animal. It was obvious that her little "Faithful" was the best of the four animals for this treacherous trip. She even enjoyed the extra thrills she received when the mule repeatedly left the muddy trail to make his own way up and down steep slopes. He had an aversion to the slippery mud, preferring to make his own hazardous trail completely oblivious to the risk of losing his rider. Eventually, she realized that her "Jefe" (Chief) had actually chosen what was best for her. By the end of the month-long trip, she had almost decided to buy him when she returned there to live.

At the end of five and a half hours over eighteen dangerous miles and across several swollen rivers, they stopped in a small mountain town at the home of Virginia Enriquez, her companion and helper in San Luis who was there for the school vacation. The next day they rode their animals for another nine hours through plateaus and up mountains until they reached Coxcatlan, the place where Leonor Soltero Ponce, Daisy's friend, came as a bride and died a year later after her baby girl was born.

It wasn't all excitement according to her own record.

> *Somewhere I met a malarial mosquito or two and so spent four days in bed of the week we were at this place. Anna and I were both so terribly tired after that day's trip, but Anna soon recovered, and I got chills and fever.*

As soon as she was able, Daisy was busy from morning until night taking care of the sick. Francisco Soltero had services each night in the adobe church filled with over three hundred people. Paul and Anna helped wherever they could and practiced their rusty Spanish learned several years before coming to Mexico.

Daisy was appalled at some of the treatments the people used for their illnesses. Without the help of a doctor or nurse or medications, they did the best they could. One little girl suffered from a burn on her arm made worse by the application of salt and vinegar and a dry clean cloth. It took many minutes of careful work to remove the cloth from the affected area in order to apply proper medication. Her heart ached for these people whose only recourse was traditional medicine based mostly on superstition.

> *I will be so glad to be able to live up here with these people. Have visions of a fine clinic and lots of medicines and instruments.*
>
> *My main feeling is a lack of knowledge. There are so many who need a doctor, will have to study hard.*
>
> *They'll have a time keeping me in San Luis after this glimpse of the needs of these people.*

The group moved from place to place through the mountains visiting market towns and villages where churches and preaching points had been established through the faithful witness of four pastors and several laymen. At each place, the pattern for their ministry was the same. Francisco Soltero preached and looked after the spiritual needs of pastor and people, while Daisy set up her portable clinic and ministered to their physical needs.

The large town of Xilitla (He-leet-la), accessible to the main road only by steep rocky trails, was especially fascinating. The main street wound along the ridge of a mountain, with small streets lined with pole and adobe houses radiating down the sides. Only one vehicle could be seen in the entire town, a Ford which had been brought up piece by piece and assembled at the top. Everything in the town was brought up on the backs of mules or men, even pianos. She wrote about their journey to Xilitla.

> *Monday's trip a hard one. We rode for about eight and a half hours over mountain trails. After a supper of chicken fearfully hot with chile, we went to a little pole church thatched with banana palms. Brother Soltero preached short which was a good thing, because the hot chile gave me rather a stomach ache.*
>
> *They put us all to bed in one room on narrow canvas cots. Brother Soltero talked in his sleep. The family cat tried to sleep under the covers with me, but I refused, so she slept on top of me which added weight and a bit of warmth, too.*

Their visit to Ahuacatlan, a twin town to Potrerillos, was expecially meaningful. This was the birthplace of all the mountain work, where Ethel and Nella True, her missionary friends from Pasadena, were saved from martyrs' deaths by a faithful Christian. The Solteros had brought them out after that encounter, feeling that the area was unsafe for single lady missionaries. By the time of Daisy's visit six years later, several more churches had been established, and the persecution was not so severe.

Daisy was filled with awe as she looked at the little house where Ethel and Nella had lived. Other stories of the early days raced through her mind, reminding her of the sacrifices which had prepared the way for her work here.

The trail to Temalacaco was the most exotic of all. Daisy was enthralled with the brightly colored parrots flying in flocks through the trees. The Indian women wore homespun clothing in a rainbow of colors and strands of matching cloth braided into their long black hair. The men were dressed in pajama-like clothing of white cotton. And once again, she was busy taking care of the sick, more than one hundred in eight hours.

Their stay in the Huasteca took them through Christmas Eve in Jalpilla and Christmas Day back in Coxcatlan. There they witnessed Christmas programs given Indian style with only male participants. From there, they retraced their steps part way to Valles in a caravan which had grown from six animals and seven people to 17 animals and 22 people. At Tancanhuitz, a bus bound for Valles replaced the animals, and finally they arrived at home in San Luis on December 29.

The trip left a lasting mark on Daisy and helped to shape her understanding of what missionary life was all about. Her eyes were opened to lifestyles and needs such as she had never seen before. She summarized the trip in a letter to her loved ones in San Diego.

> *I saw about 400 patients, did what I could for each. It made my heart ache over and over again to have those poor people come and not know what to do for them. How I wish I were a doctor.*
>
> *Also, we need more preachers — and we need to train our own — and there is no money coming in to train those we would like to have. Twelve dollars and fifty cents will take care of each boy's room, board, and expenses a month. . . . What can we do? We brought 3 little girls and Virginia and another older girl, 3 little boys and 5 older boys with us. At least 6 more are coming next week.*
>
> *I love these people more than ever.*

Moved by the desperate need of the people they had visited, and their lack of finance and workers with which to meet that need, the little band of missionaries began to pray earnestly for the Huasteca. They asked for more workers to be called, and adequate provisions for their training. They sought God's leadership for the next step in reaching their part of Mexico with the gospel.

Part III

The Ministry Years
Surprises and Sacrifices

"God never wastes a consecrated life. Somehow, some way, in every circumstance, He will use that life to His praise."

Bertha Monroe

Chapter 8

Where Needed Most

San Luis or San Diego

Delight thyself also in the Lord; and he shall give thee the desires of thine heart. Commit thy way unto the Lord; trust also in him; and he shall bring it to pass. . . . Rest in the Lord, and wait patiently for him. . . . (Psalm 37:4-5, 7 KJV).

Coming back to the routine of life in the big house in San Luis from the emotional high of the trip to the mountains took some renewed dedication for Daisy. It wasn't where she wanted to be, but it was where she had to be for the time being. It would have been easy for her to stumble into the slough of despond, but she had learned long ago that it was best to do what one had to do with a willing heart.

You should see our room — we have every inch occupied it seems. Have 4 beds in this room besides 3 chairs, my large desk, 3 trunks, 2 suitcases on boxes as places for clothes, dresser, large wash stand, small wash stand, stove, and 3 shelves with curtains around for clothes, and my medicine cupboard and seven girls.

We expect 2 more girls next week so will probably move our little girls to another room to sleep, and then they can be put to bed on time and we big school girls will have time to study at night. We have a fine electric light here.

Being Mamacita to nine girls from the Huasteca consumed her time and energy. The girls' ages ranged from 7 to 19, which meant that they were in nine different stages of personal development and school from the elementary grades to college. The youngest needed constant watching, because her natural curiosity sent her exploring every nook and cranny of her new home. Two of the younger girls were sometimes weepy with homesickness. And to top it all off, Mamacita Daisy found her Spanish vocabulary sometimes lacking in "mothering" words.

That was missionary life, and Daisy accepted it cheerfully. This was where she was "needed most" at the moment, and she was determined to do whatever it took to be a good team missionary for Jesus and for those in her care. Those two concepts governing her attitudes toward her missionary assignments took root during those early years and remained a part of her commitment all her life.

The Solteros supervised eleven boys who also lived in the big house. Nettie managed the kitchen with the help of a good cook, taught the boys how to keep themselves and their clothing clean, helped them with their school work, and taught Bible school at night to those who felt called to preach.

Francisco supervised their outside chores, pastored the local Pilgrim church, and was district superintendent for the eleven churches and eleven preaching points located around San Luis and in the Huasteca. He gave constant guidance to the four preachers and many lay workers in the district, and managed an extensive literature distribution program. He gave supervision to the Grouts as they tried to learn Mexican ways and taught classes in the Bible school.

Even as the busy days blended together in a blur of activity, the vision of the Huasteca lifted Daisy's inner spirit. If and when she returned to the Huasteca to live, she needed to know more about the illnesses of these people and how to treat them, especially when there would be no doctor to lean on. Daisy decided that the waiting period should be used to improve her nursing skills.

With the Solteros' permission, she enrolled in classes in the Institute in San Luis along with some of her girls. She was assured by the doctor who taught one of her classes that she would be able to finish all the lacking requirements for a degree in nursing in addition to her diploma within one year. She was especially thrilled when she brought the textbook home and discovered that she could read and understand the Spanish.

By summertime, the overworked team of missionaries was almost to the breaking point. Added to the stress of constant work was the continuing lack of funds. Finally it was decided that Nettie Soltero should go to the United States to tell their story in an effort to raise money. Daisy was suddenly thrust into the role of mother of the entire family as well as nurse for the community. The load was bearable because she knew that Mrs.

Soltero would be home by the end of summer and that even before she returned, her nurse friend from Pasadena, Mrs. Rilla Chapman, would be arriving to join the team. God gave her grace from day to day so that she was able to write victoriously to her Papa.

> *Dear Papacito,*
>
> *This is such an interesting country that I believe you would see why I have no desire to go back to live in the States. Why shouldn't I make good here, with the influence of Christian parents and grandparents as I've had and a clear call to the mission field and a big God who helps me over every difficulty?*

There were happy, satisfying times in the big house. Daisy's heart swelled with pride just like any mother's when her daughters danced around their big room outfitted in new dresses she made for them. Each time one was finished, she secretly thanked the Lord for prompting her to take that sewing class so long ago. She delighted in spending her time and money on her Mexican family, some of whom had only one change of clothing when they arrived. In fact, she gave to them almost to the exclusion of any concern for herself.

After several months, her "children" began to realize that their Mamacita was neglecting herself for their sakes. Virginia, the oldest who had been with her from the beginning, knew that it would do no good to insist that she make something for herself. So she encouraged her "sisters" to talk about how tired they were of seeing her in her three green uniforms. Daisy was convinced when one of them declared, "I see nothing but green when I'm awake, and I dream green at night."

Nursing, sewing, helping with homework, guiding cooks and cleaners and managing household finances, plus hours spent in just plain listening took their toll on Daisy. She didn't realize how tired she was until Mrs. Chapman arrived and began to help, especially with the nursing. Only then did she begin to dream again about going to the mountains. Would it be in November or next year in March or April?

Mrs. Soltero returned from the north, and as things began to return to normal, Daisy was sent to Valles for a much needed vacation of two weeks. Even though she was so close, she never reached any of the mountain towns where her heart longed to be.

Back in San Luis, the missionaries met every afternoon to pray for the money to make the final payments on their property and for direction in planning for the ongoing of the work. Many different strategies were discussed. One of those plans would turn the work in San Luis over to the Grouts and Miss Chapman, with the Solteros and Daisy moving down to Valles where they could more easily do the medical work, Bible school, and superintend the exploding work in the Huasteca.

Then suddenly with the beginning of 1930, changes happened so fast that Daisy's head was swimming. The Grouts decided not to remain in the Mexican work. The girls and Daisy were moved out of the big house to a smaller rented one nearby. Then in one month the girls were all sent home because of lack of funds to feed and care for them. It was decided to concentrate their efforts on the church, Bible school, and the nursing ministry. Rilla Chapman and Daisy were moved back to the little house on the property where Grouts had been, and Solteros and twenty-two young men who came back from vacation occupied the big house.

Even then, she was sure she would go to the Huasteca in February, but February came and went, and she could not go. Her days were full of sewing, serving, helping with the church work, and nursing.

Added to Daisy's anxiety about her continuing ministry in Mexico was an agonizing feeling that all was not well at home. Each letter from her mother brought news of fewer jobs in the building trade as the depression deepened in the United States. That meant little work for her father. There were also severe testings in the family. She found herself searching for scriptures for them to read, and writing long exhortations to keep trusting the God who never fails. Once she preached them a little sermon on Psalm 55:22, "Cast thy burden upon the Lord, and he shall sustain thee."

She was preaching what she was trying to practice. Mexican government restrictions on ministers and missionaries from the United States were steadily being tightened. The monthly support from the missionary department was always late and often far short of the promised amount as the economic troubles grew more severe at home. It became increasingly difficult to stretch the money to include Daisy who was still not a "regular" missionary, and individual contributions for her were becoming less and less. In the meantime, the work continued to grow so rapidly that they did not see how anyone could be spared from the team.

Abruptly, at the end of August 1930, Daisy was called away from Mexico to the United States to raise money for the work. The Great Depression was on, and giving declined to a trickle as people in the home church struggled with unemployment. She visited relatives in Michigan, gave her missionary story about Mexico more than fifty times in Michigan, Ohio, Indiana, Kentucky, and Colorado, and found herself at home in San Diego by Christmas.

It was wonderful to be home, but Daisy had left her heart in Mexico. She knew she was "called," but maybe this was where she was needed most for now. Her very nature was to be busy, and she was determined not to sit and wait for something to happen. Daisy immediately resumed her place in the family almost as if she'd never been away, bringing cheer and comfort to her parents. Daisy was like a breath of fresh air around the house, always sharing interesting experiences from her two years in Mexico, and always reassuring family and friends that God would provide.

As soon as word spread that Daisy was at home and available for nursing, calls for her help began to come. She accepted these joyfully, believing that God was giving her a way to earn and save for the future. Every spare dollar was saved. And she was asked to speak about Mexico in churches all over southern California. Because she could now speak Spanish fluently, there were many opportunities to share Jesus with Mexicans around her, and also across the border in Ensenada. Her testimony to the "Robins" revealed the disciplined exercise of patience while waiting.

> *Still in San Diego, nursing, helping out where I can and waiting as patiently as I can for the time to come when I can return to my dear Mexicans and Aztecs. Surely the Lord has been with me and blessed me.*

Sometime during the second year, she received a letter from the Solteros explaining that they along with the home board had concluded that it seemed unwise to continue the development of the Bible school property in San Luis. Government was threatening to take over church properties and had already passed laws prohibiting American missionaries to reside in Mexico and do their work. They were moving to a rented property in Laredo, Texas.

They would continue to travel to Mexico to supervise the work and have short institutes, but the main school work would be in Texas. In addition, they would seek to develop a Texas border district of American-Mexican churches. She knew that already Paul and Anna Grout had established a church there while Paul taught school to support themselves and the project. The news breathed new life into her determination to return to the Mexican work. A glimmer of light began to shine at the end of the long tunnel of waiting.

Early in 1933, she was asked to participate in a missionary convention in Pasadena. Talking about the work and hearing other missionaries tell of theirs brought back the intense longing to join her colleagues on the Texas border. During those months, she also formed a friendship with Flora Belle Slater who would become her co-worker in years to come. At that point, she didn't even know how to spell her name.

During the convention, Seth Rees crumbled under the weight of church leadership and a worsening heart ailment. She was asked to take care of him. After two weeks of very intense day and night nursing, he regained strength and she was released to care for another very important person in her life.

A call came from Los Angeles that Francisco Soltero's mother was at the point of death and was calling for her. She went immediately and gave her several weeks of loving care. And Mother Soltero recovered!

The rewards to Daisy for those weeks were twofold — she had the joy of using her Spanish, and the grateful old mother wrote to her son that anyone who could speak Spanish like that and was such a good nurse really belonged in Mexico. The Soltero's letter of thanks to Daisy urged her to return to the Mexican work very soon, adding fuel to the fire already burning in her heart.

However, she could not escape from the sense that she was still "needed most" in Pasadena for a little while longer, because Seth Rees's condition continued to deteriorate. The family pleaded with her to move into the house to take care of him.

April 9

Dear Friends of the Nest,

I came to live at Rees' and have been here now over 6 weeks. At times it has seemed that Bro. Rees wouldn't live overnight, and at other times he has been stronger. . . . It has been a long hard strain on all (the family) especially on Bro. Rees because he has always been so cheerful throughout these days, and at times when he seemed the nearest death he has kept us laughing with his dry wit.

He calls me his "Popish" nurse. I have a sign on the front gate informing the general public that he must see no one. He told me that I should put on that sign, "To see the sick, consult the Pope."

He told Brother Paul Thomas that I've never once remembered that he is General Superintendent of the Pilgrim Church.

March 10. I am helping to get some of Bro. Rees' sermons corrected for the Advocate. And the ones that have been in I've clipped and put together in order. It is quite a job.

Bro. Rees preached a real sermon to me on Romans 1:16 last Sunday a.m. — 35 minutes long.

April 1. Bro. Rees continues to fail. He almost left us today, but now after a stimulant, he is a bit stronger. I do not believe he will be here longer than Monday anyway. He is so funny at times and keeps us laughing even when he is sickest.

What would you say if I decided to go to Mexico inside of 2 weeks? I'm seriously considering it. I want to go for the Assembly if at all possible.

April 20. Paul, Edith and Evangeline were to have left for Detroit last Monday, but have decided to wait now until next month. Dr. Wagner says he can't promise that Bro. Rees will ever be any stronger, and he says that anything might take him. He thinks that the perfect nursing care is what has kept him as long as he has been here. Pat myself on the back!!

April 26. Bro. Rees continues about the same, some days a bit better and other days not so good.

The Mexican Assembly begins today. How wonderful it would have been if I could have been there at Valles!

August 18. I was with Brother Rees until his homegoing on May 22nd just at the break of day. His death was a translation. He suffered a great deal those last few weeks and was unconscious when the end came — but his going was very peaceful.

The homegoing of Seth C. Rees concluded a significant era in Daisy's life. It seemed to her that the birthing process for The Pilgrim Church and her own missionary career were finished when he died. He was the person whom God used more than any other to prepare her spiritually and mentally for missionary service. She was honored that God, in His providence, allowed her to be there when he and his family needed her.

Could it be that now, God would allow her to go back to actually being a missionary?

Daisy cares for Billie

Left to right: Daisy, Papa, Nelson, Mama, Janie, Alvin, Bill

A nurse at last

Some of the "Robins"

The sure-footed mule

Co-workers, Daisy and Flora Belle

Improvising in Puerto Rico

San Ignacio, the church that faith built —
Faithful member, Daisy, and
Martha Hahn

Mexican Bible School group in San Antonio
Francisco Soltero in center, Mrs. Soltero to his left with Daisy beside her

Summer Bible School for young women in
Ciudad Valles. Rachel Torres (Vega) in center
of front row with Mrs. Soltero to her left and
Daisy to her right

Daisy with her dear
friend and mentor, Mrs.
Nettie Soltero

Flora Belle and Daisy on trek through the
mountains of Mexico

*Daisy and Minnie in
Puerto Rico*

*Puerto Rico Bible School family — Rachel and
Andres Vega (from Mexico) on Daisy's left*

*The happy president of the
Peruvian Bible Institute*

*Daisy's Peruvian Bible Institute family.
Daisy in middle of third row.*

*A ministerial graduate from Peruvian
Bible Institute*

*Mr. and Mrs. Jose Molina
in Puerto Rico — Daisy's
God-given helpers*

Helping out at Wesleyan Bible College in the Philippine — Daisy beside Flora Belle Slater in front row.

Working with Filipino missionaries, the Pantangans, in Indonesia.

Preaching through interpreter in Indonesia

Final retirement home in Brooksville, Florida

Reminders of the past in their retirement home.

A servant at heart 'til the end — Caring for Flora Belle

Chapter 9

A Missionary Again

To San Ygnacio

He calleth his own sheep by name, and leadeth them out. When he hath put forth all his own, he goeth before them, and the sheep follow him; for they know his voice (John 10:3-4 KJV).

Shimmering heat waves danced above the parched ground as summer came to an end. It was the kind of oppressively hot day in late August when many Californians escaped to the ocean or looked for a cool spot in the shade. But not Daisy nor the Grout family. They crowded into the Grout's car to begin the long journey from San Diego to Laredo. Daisy's belongings were packed into a small open trailer hitched to the car. After a vacation with loved ones in Pasadena, the Grouts were returning to their new church in Lyford on the Texas border. Daisy was joining the Solteros in Laredo after three long years with her missionary career on hold.

An intense struggle raged in Daisy's heart as the summer months of 1933 came and went. The desire to return to the Mexican work filled nearly all her waking moments. The missionary board could not support her when she went the first time, and once again the lack of money kept her off the list of board-appointed missionaries. The big question was how to determine whether her strong desire was pushing her into presumption, or whether God was really saying once more, "Go and trust me." She prayed earnestly for some unmistakable evidence that it was God's time for her to go back.

The first glimmer of divine direction came when several people promised to send her money. The second positive sign came when Paul and Anna suggested that she might travel to Laredo with them. Again, she had to know that this was God's provision and not just the kindness of people who offered to help out

71

of pity for her. As a child of God, Daisy refused to be known as "poor, dear Daisy." If she went, she would go triumphantly in the confidence that God would take care of her.

As she waited on the Lord, He gave her a command and a promise, ". . . Go your way, eat the fat, and drink the sweet, and send portions unto them for whom nothing is prepared: for this day is holy unto our Lord: neither be ye sorry; for the joy of the Lord is your strength" (Nehemiah 8:10 KJV). That meant "GO" to Daisy. If she had enough to be able to give to others after she had eaten herself, surely there would be plenty.

Her decision was severely tested even before embarking on the journey to Laredo. Some of her supporters withdrew their promises. Once again, she went to the Lord and His Word for confirmation. This time God showed her more "Fear nots" in His Word than she had realized were there, and every one seemed to be for her. She knew God would never fail to keep His promises, so she packed her things and went. Even the catastrophes which befell them along the way did not shake her confidence.

A wheel came off the trailer and hurtled on down among the rocks just as they descended a long grade into the Imperial Desert. After several minutes of diligent searching, the wheel was found and put back in place. Later the trailer hitch broke, necessitating a long delay in the stifling heat as well as unexpected costs for repairs. Before the journey ended, their patience was tested again when they had a flat tire during a heavy rain storm. Finally, the exhausted little family and Daisy were welcomed with outstretched arms by the Solteros and others in Laredo. Daisy was back — with only $2.00 in her pocket!

Word spread rapidly that Nurse Daisy had arrived, so immediately people came with their illnesses. Within days she was busy with nursing cases and feeling like a missionary again. Now and then, someone pressed money into her hand in gratitude for her loving service. God was showing her that He would take care of her.

Two weeks after she arrived, the Solteros invited her to go with them to San Ygnacio, a small Mexican town on the Texas side of the Rio Grande. Laredo and San Ygnacio were linked by 15 miles of beautiful blacktop highway which ended abruptly in 20 more miles of corrugated dirt road. A new church was being planted in this town of 700 inhabitants set among rolling hills covered with mesquite trees and cactus. A few irrigated ranches in the surrounding countryside provided vegetables for the city of Laredo.

The homes were either stone or weather-beaten, unpainted wooden structures. The yards, completely without grass, were swept clean. A few flowers planted in tin cans provided bright splashes of color amidst the drab surroundings. The only running water in the community was in the river. It was brought to the homes in two-wheeled horse-drawn carts loaded with two 50-gallon drums. Daisy noted that there was electricity in the town, but not in all the homes.

The church had been started by a faithful lay preacher, Alberto Uresti, who butchered and sold meat to all the ranches and small villages along the Rio Grande river road. On his return he would stop and hold services by the light of a lantern hung in a tree or on the front of a building. He preached to crowds of men and boys where the people invited him, or more often where he invited himself. By the time Daisy arrived in Laredo, a small group of believers was ready for someone to live among them and have services on a more permanent basis.

Daisy was surprised to see that there were only two or three women and two little girls among the crowd of men in that first service she attended. The rented building was packed, and many more Mexicans stood outside, curious but reluctant to enter a Protestant place of worship. The response to Francisco's dynamic preaching that night revealed the deep spiritual hunger among the people.

Daisy's heart told her what was coming as they drove back to Laredo after the service. Francisco Soltero presented his plan to her as they bumped along the dirt road with the dust swirling around them. Would she consider coming to San Ygnacio to be their missionary and take care of their sick? It didn't take long for her to accept. She had already fallen in love with the place and people, deeply moved with compassion over their physical and spiritual needs. By the time they reached the smooth paved highway, the dream of nursing in the Huasteca changed to visions of ministry in the Rio Grande Valley. As time passed, Daisy came to think of that fifteen miles of blacktop road as one of the luxuries of her life on the Texas border.

Plans developed rapidly for the move to San Ygnacio. It was arranged that a volunteer single lady preacher from Indiana who had some support would work with Daisy to assist with the preaching. With dismay, Daisy later discovered that her "support" consisted of $5.00 a month. She concluded that this next chapter in her missionary career was definitely going to be a faith venture.

> *Miss Hardin and I moved to San Ygnacio and rented one half of a large stone house for $1.00 a month. Brother Soltero put up a partition made of wood framing with cretonne (heavy cloth) tacked to it since the whole house was only one large room. When cold weather came, we would close our doors against the penetrating north winds, light the kerosene lamp, fill a hot water bottle for each of us, and sit at the table to study.*
>
> *We cooked on a one-burner oil stove which sat on a packing box that Brother Soltero had equipped with shelves made from the cover. Our larder was a 100-pound lard can which kept the mice and roaches out of our food. Brother Soltero put up a shelf in the corner with a rod under it for our wardrobe. We hung a curtain around it. Our table was home made, and our rocker and two straight chairs were loaned to us. One of those chairs went to pieces one day like the "one horse shay."*
>
> *The church which was rented for $2.00 a month was two short blocks away. It was equipped with a squeaky folding organ, a very simple pulpit, an altar, and a few benches.*

Daisy rested in the promise God gave as she began her work in San Ygnacio. "Be not afraid, but speak, and hold not thy peace, for I am with thee, and no man shall sit on thee to hurt thee, for I have much people in this city," Acts 18:9-10. Even in the face of strong opposition from the Catholic priest, she prayed and testified fearlessly in the homes of the people.

Very soon, Daisy and Norma moved to a larger house where they used the living room for church and lived in three small rooms at the back for themselves. There were twenty-five believers ready to be received as charter members, and Daisy's fame had spread abroad as a successful nurse and midwife. The two missionaries lived on the small proceeds from Daisy's baby deliveries augmented by love gifts of vegetables and fruit brought in by the grateful church people. Now and then they received a small gift from "home." The rented house church overflowed with 80 regular attenders and many more for special events.

Almost immediately Daisy preached to her small congregation that they must purchase their own land and build their own church. If the Indians in the mountains of Mexico could do it, then surely these people could. One old Mexican lady responded the very next morning with an offering of fifty cents to buy the first board or the first stone. It was small, but it was a beautiful, sacrificial demonstration of her love for her missionaries and her church. It was followed by many others.

Before that year was over, Norma married a young man from the area who was called to preach. They went to Laredo to join the Bible school in order for him to prepare for the ministry. Her replacement was a new missionary from California, Flora Belle Slater, her friend from Pasadena, the daughter of missionaries who had served in the Caribbean and Africa.

Flora Belle told their mutual friends in a Round Robin letter about her first home with Daisy.

> *We laugh often and a great deal. You know me, I couldn't live without a good many laughs. One of our best this week was the day we invented steam heat for our room. It had suddenly grown quite cold. We had the little kitchen oil stove on, but it didn't seem to be doing much good. We had sat down to our little table to have our Bible study, but were so cold we couldn't keep our minds on the topic. How about putting the stove under the table? No sooner said than done! But the heat from the burner would spoil our new oilcloth. So onto the burner the teakettle went. The steam felt good, but that would warp the wood. So onto the spout a little cup went. But the steam condensed and dropped on the floor and made it wet. So under the cup a little pan went. And thus, girls, was invented the first steam-heated house in San Ygnacio.*
>
> *We have entirely abandoned our big room since there is no possible way to heat it, and are cramped up in the two tiny rooms at the rear. But it is cozy even though it would send an interior decorator absolutely mad. . . . The blue calcimined walls are kind of scaly, but they are better than the partition of cretonne, for it goes only half way to the high ceiling. We can hear even the lowest conversation of the Mexicans on the other side. Since we have the brightest light, they can see everything we do at night.*
>
> *It is rather difficult to bathe in the dark, especially when we have to use the little wash basin. But I'll tell you, there is one good thing about having the other part of the bathroom outside. One always has to dress the first thing in the morning, and then you always get to see the stars and sometimes the moon the last thing at night.*

The days were filled with visiting the sick, delivering babies, talking to people about Jesus, and preaching. Their trips over the roadless countryside were made on horseback or by walking. Sometimes, a frantic rancher would come for them in his rickety truck, hauling them through rocky riverbeds and over bumpy fields to care for a sick family member. They dubbed those trips "auto broncoing." It was nothing unusual to visit ten house patients a day, and to care for another fifty in their parsonage home. Under their combined ministry, the little church flourished, and the building fund grew.

One of Solteros' assignments for Daisy that year was to teach Spanish to her new co-worker. Daisy was an excellent teacher, and Flora Belle was an apt learner. The setting was ideal for learning Spanish since very few people in San Ygnacio spoke English. Perhaps they were too successful. In ten months, Flora Belle was called to Laredo to teach in the Bible school and in the summer institute in Valles.

Daisy's next assigned helper was Miss Marie Stocker, a Swiss missionary affectionately known as Stocky. During Stocky's time with her, they were able to buy a lot on the main street into town on which to build the church. The lot was made available by an interested resident for $40.00, and they were able to pay cash. It was the great miracle of 1935!

Stocky taught Daisy to forget her abhorrence of the muddy water in the Rio Grande, enough to plunge in for a swim and bath during the summer months when the thermometer rose to 110 degrees or higher. At first, all Daisy could think about was the mud which settled into the bottom of their water tank after each filling from the river. But eventually, she decided if Stocky could enjoy cooling off in the filthy water, she could too.

The two of them began making plans that summer to build their church. Daisy wrote to her father for suggestions and a drawing, giving him the dimensions of the lot and a description of the lay of the land. In early fall, everything was ready except the money even though the church people were giving all they could.

Two big surprises put the San Ygnacio building project on hold. One was Soltero's decision to move from Laredo to San Antonio. Daisy was called to help the Solteros, Flora Belle, and others to move the Bible school and headquarters to the new location.

Back in San Ygnacio one month later, she received the shock of her life. A letter from the missionary office in Indianapolis called for her to come north to tell about the Mexican work across the church. They would pay all her traveling expenses plus $30.00 a month. It wasn't the money that enticed her, or the opportunity to travel. It was the thought that at last, she would be a "real" board-appointed missionary about to be put on contract by the department even if it was only to be a "returned" missionary. She accepted the assignment and arrived in Indianapolis in late November.

Daisy loaded her suitcases on and off buses and trains for the next five months. She told her Mexican story in the churches of Michigan, Ohio, and Indiana. The people responded well to this lovely, thoughtful missionary lady with the happy face and the dancing blue eyes. She told her parents in a letter from Winchester, Indiana, "I have received a lot of compliments on my speaking. Have to watch not to get the 'big head.' The Lord has helped me so much."

Nonetheless, she was thrilled when she was released to go back to her home in San Ygnacio by way of San Diego. She was back in time to go to the Assembly in Valles before settling back into the routine of life on the border.

When Daisy returned to San Ygnacio, she found another helper. Martha Hahn, her dear friend and classmate from Pasadena Bible school and nursing school days, had been sent to carry on in her absence. Martha had already served in the Mexican work and dearly loved the people. The nursing tasks as well as the church work could now be divided between them.

Sometimes Daisy wished fervently that she had become a doctor when some of the physical problems of her people taxed all her knowledge and training. At times, she went to Laredo to consult with a public health doctor about difficult medical cases. On one of those visits, he offered her a social service job at $120 a month. She told her mother about it.

> *I told him that I was afraid he couldn't get me for that. I might have told him that if I'd wanted money, I'd stayed in California where I could make more. Anyway, I'm needed here in San Ygnacio, and I wouldn't get out of the Lord's will for any amount.*

Daisy and Martha desperately wanted to build the new church and parsonage. The growing congregation needed the stability and identity that their own church building would give them. As the townspeople became interested in the project and began to offer their help for the work, they decided the time had come. They would trust God to provide the lacking funds as they proceeded. Daisy told the "girls" in the Round Robin about it.

*These have been such busy months since we broke
ground for our church and parsonage on May 25th (1937).
We had hoped to have a competent carpenter to oversee the
building, but it was impossible, so with homemade plans in
one hand and a rule in the other, yours truly went forth to
be contractor and builder. The men were wonderful to help.
There are mistakes and misfits, but everyone had a mind to
work, and we can overlook a great deal. (None of us will
have a perfectly built house until we reach heaven anyway.)
The church is 24 x 36, and has a corrugated sheet iron roof
and dirt floor. We hope to get the cement in before
Christmas.*

*The house is attached at the rear with the front door
opening toward the street. There are two large rooms that
will be divided Mexican style with cretonne partitions into
4. All with cement floor laid. We have screens on windows
and screen doors, and 4 of our 8 windows are in.*

*We began with $147 cash, have spent over $500, and
only owe $75 now, and that without interest, payable when
we wish. We are truly happy, for it is no less than a miracle.*

The church was built during a severe drought in the Rio
Grande Valley. The usual rains had not come for more than a
year, and the parched ground could not be cultivated. Many of
the townspeople helped with the building since they could not
work in their fields. Their only vegetables came from the irrigated ranches in the area. Water was so scarce that the town's supply from the shrinking river had to be rationed.

Necessity demanded that Daisy and Martha learn to recycle
this precious commodity. They made a small basin of bath
water do triple duty. After the bath, it was used for washing the
clothing they had worn that day and then was poured on the
few plants and flowers around their house.

On the day of dedication, the priest told his congregation
that since they had helped build the church, it wouldn't rain for
a whole year more. He had scarcely driven out of town when it
began to rain — hard! The noise was so deafening on the corrugated iron roof that it was impossible to hear the preacher.
Everyone in the congregation was smiling with great satisfaction. They knew of the priest's prediction, although Daisy and
Martha did not until after the service.

It rained so hard that the streets were flooded, and everyone
left the church to walk home with their shoes in their hands

instead of on their feet. No one minded the inconvenience. The rain continued most of that day and every day for a week. There was no doubt in the minds of the people of San Ygnacio that this first little Protestant church in their town was the work of God.

It was a struggle to finish the church, but the work went on as funds became available. Windows, floors, and even proper furniture were needed. If Daisy thought she was busy before, she was now pressed beyond measure.

> *This is some life! Making cement floors, delivering babies, preaching sermons, moving, sifting sand, entertaining visitors, getting meals, washing clothes and dishes, preparing lists of lumber and cement needed for the next load from Laredo, selling five cents of aspirin or a purgative, mending and keeping Martha out of mischief, helping a neighbor change her clothes line, etc. Do you wonder my mind is in a whirl?*

Daisy's life in San Ygnacio was sprinkled with trips to Mexico, delightful respite from the grinding work load. Visitors also brightened Daisy's simple mission home during those six years on the border. Paul Thomas, general secretary of the missions department, friends from Pasadena, Mrs. Seth Rees, and others received hospitality fit for kings and queens. Perhaps the most joyfully received among her visitors were Mama and Papa Buby, each at different times. Their coming somehow validated her missionary work for her family, and made it easier for them to visualize Daisy among "her Mexicans."

Chapter 10

A New Assignment

Daisy Becomes a Teacher

Remember ye not the former things, neither consider the things of old. Behold, I will do a new thing; now it shall spring forth; shall ye not know it? (Isaiah 43:18-19a KJV).

D oes God ever make a mistake? Daisy was quite sure God didn't, but when she read the letter from the secretary of world missions, the Reverend Paul Thomas, she wondered if perhaps the missions department did. They were suggesting that she might be needed to do deputation again — soon! She mused, "They must be really hard up for speakers to call me again. Surely they won't go through with this. I'm not that good at it."

That letter came late in September 1938. She had a month to get used to the idea of another round of travel before the second letter came with her schedule and clergy book for obtaining discounted train and bus fares. Her first service would be in Buffalo, New York, on November 8.

Once again, Daisy dutifully packed her suitcases with her "speaking clothes," turned her beloved work and people in San Ygnacio over to Martha, and started off for the cold northland. Life became an adventure that winter, rushing to catch trains or buses, traveling over snow and ice in order to fulfill speaking engagements. The more pleasant part of the task was being welcomed by old friends and making new ones. She spoke twenty-seven times in the first twenty-four days, while facing a second grueling schedule of forty-two places to be covered in thirty-six days. She was in and out of headquarters in Indianapolis or the homes of her relatives in Michigan.

By March of the next year, she was eagerly looking forward to discarding her worn-out winter clothing. As usual, she shared her thoughts with Mama.

My clothes look like spring should be here. My over-
shoes are wearing out, my outing (flannel) nightgown you
got me last winter has had to have 2 tears sewed up. It's all
I have and doesn't look too encouraging. And my hat looks
as though it should be retired on pension. When I get into
Pittsburgh next week, I expect to do some buying. The mis-
sionary should look well-dressed!

She crisscrossed the eastern one third of the country until
the end of September that year with a one-month break to visit
Mexico and San Ygnacio. Those ten and a half long months of
living out of suitcases finally ended with a challenging new
assignment for Daisy. Flora Belle Slater was to come from San
Antonio to take over her deputation work, and Daisy was asked
to take her place. The wonder of it was that she was to receive
regular support — $26.00 a month.

The first order of business upon returning to Texas was to
explain the turn of events to the folks in San Ygnacio. They
accepted the decisions of their leaders reluctantly when they
understood that the change was necessary because Mrs. Soltero
was ill and had to have help. She packed her belongings and
went back to San Antonio. Her next home was a small rented
house where she was to live with yet another new co-worker,
Sarah May Rooker, secretary to Mr. Soltero.

San Antonio, Texas
October 9, 1939

Dear Robins,

I'm back again among my Mexicans, but in a new
capacity, now as teacher in our Bible School, and I know I'm
going to enjoy it so much.

How I did enjoy visiting camp meetings this summer,
was in 12 different ones, and though the traveling was quite
tiring, yet I would not have missed them. I enjoyed meeting
the Pilgrims over the U.S.A. and others, too. I spent 10 1/2
months in this work, traveled over 23,000 miles, or an aver-
age of a little better than 500 miles per week for 45 weeks,
was in 7 missionary Rallies, 1 youth convention, 12 camps,
and spoke 273 times in 143 churches and 6 schools.

But oh! how good it seems to be settled again, not hav-
ing to pack and unpack and rush for trains.

I will carry a very heavy teaching program for the next 6

months with 12 very interesting students, 9 of them Aztec Indians. It is all new to me, but I got a real thrill yesterday a.m. as I listened to those boys give their testimonies. Their earnestness was so splendid. They are alive and full of mischief for the most part and make us laugh quite frequently by their comments. One boy said to the others (they eat by themselves and enjoy it), "Don't serve yourself too much. You won't like this new cooking at first. I didn't last year when I came!"

The work is growing so fast that our second year boys could not return this year for their third year. They had to stay by the stuff.

Daisy's nursing equipment took second place to a stack of books, a chalkboard, and a grade book. She taught five classes including Theology, Spanish grammar, Life of Christ, Bible classes, and Mexican history. And she took care of the ailments of the Bible school family besides.

Preparing lessons for classes made up of young people at different educational levels was a real challenge. Some were learning and using Spanish, their medium of instruction, for the first time. The teachers shared techniques which they had found effective in helping their students learn. One of them was to prepare picture handouts to illustrate their lessons. Daisy wrote home several times that year about the challenge of seeing that her students really learned their material. She adopted a quote from Isaiah as her theme, "For precept must be upon precept, precept upon precept; line upon line, line upon line; here a little, and there a little" (Isaiah 28:10).

Grading test papers was a challenge, too. Many of their students had never taken written tests since many village schools in those days were done by rote. When he couldn't think of the answer to a question, one student would write, "Mind does not recall." Further down on the paper he would write, "Mind does recall," and would proceed with an answer. It was up to the teacher to figure out which "does recall" went with which "does not recall."

She hadn't counted on one of her extra curricular assignments. Solteros felt that all their young pastors should know how to play a musical instrument whether or not they had ability. Since accordions were more portable than organs, and some had been donated by friends for the Mexican work, several chose to learn the accordion. Daisy discovered that sometimes missionary teachers were obliged to teach things they had never studied, namely accordion! She managed to teach herself first — enough to keep ahead of her students — and secretly thanked the Lord for her years of piano lessons.

By this time, Daisy knew from experience that missionaries are constantly thrust into new situations, but she was learning that she was never quite prepared for them. During the final months of that year, she was left alone and in charge of the students while Solteros and Flora Belle (having a brief respite from deputation) went to conduct the customary institute for girls in Valles. It was a heavy responsibility which demanded all the grace and wisdom she could muster. She came through two months with flying colors, and without the loss of a single student. It was important to her that Solteros pronounced her a super teacher and manager.

School closing came at the end of March and everyone prepared for the Mexican District Assembly. On the appointed day in April, two station wagons, fifteen passengers including the Reverend Paul Thomas and Flora Belle, and mounds of baggage embarked on the 700-mile journey from San Antonio southward to Ciudad Valles.

For the first time in the history of the work, Francisco Soltero was unable to go to the assembly. The doctor and Mr. Thomas pronounced him too ill to make the trip and sent him off to a lovely Colorado ranch owned by Pilgrims for a complete rest. Even while protesting the plan, Francisco admitted that he had pushed himself too far and was at the end of his strength. He agreed to go, trusting his plan for the advancement of the work to his wife and other workers. The historic assembly adopted his five-year plan for doubling every aspect of the work in time for the twenty-fifth anniversary in 1945.

Following the conference, Daisy and Flora Belle helped Nettie Soltero with the girls' institute and a ministerial convention in Valles with visits to the mountain churches in between. By the time Daisy arrived back in San Antonio, she was exhausted. And then it happened again! Another stint of deputation! The department agreed to send her home to California for a rest before bringing her to West Virginia for a heavy schedule of meetings. Then Kentucky, and Ohio, and back home to San Antonio for Christmas.

While Daisy was away from San Antonio that time, a shocking development concerning the Bible school forced the Mexican missionary family to revise their plans for training students. The Mexican government refused to allow the young people to go across the border unless the school would be accredited. Their immediate solution was to have their Bible school classes in Valles which meant that the American teachers had to reside in San Antonio and travel to Mexico for short school sessions. Even though it meant having school in less than ideal buildings, the enrollment increased from twenty-five to sixty-eight students in three years.

Daisy spent the next four years like a yo-yo at the end of a string — a few months in the north for deputation — down through San Antonio to Valles for a few months in Bible Institute — then back north for deputation. She became a "pro" at both pursuits, being much in demand as a missionary speaker and much-loved as a teacher.

Those were the war years, so travel became increasingly difficult. Daisy made her trips by train, since bus travel was restricted by gasoline rationing. The trains were crowded with servicemen and civilians and were almost always late. Often she had to sit in the vestibule of a car on her suitcase until a seat inside would be vacated. She hated with a passion the stinking cigar and cigarette smoke that filled those small closed areas.

The hardships of the journey were put aside when she arrived at her destination to be warmly welcomed by pastors and people. Her heart burned with the stories of her beloved Mexican work, and she told them with quiet, captivating intensity. They were stories well worth telling, for the work was growing and people were coming to know Jesus through the ministry of the young men and women being trained in their school. Daisy was not a dramatic speaker, but she painted word pictures from the heart. It is no wonder that she became one of the most sought-after deputation speakers.

One of her favorite stories was about Luis Villareal, a young Aztec pastor. When he came to Bible school, he discovered that all students were required to learn and speak Spanish. Because it was so difficult for him, he would give his testimony in Aztec if given the slightest opportunity. The faculty decided that the testimony was what really counted, not the language in which it was given.

"Before I became a Christian, I wanted to have a Pinto horse, a saddle decorated with real silver, silver spurs, a big sombrero (hat), and a pistol. But when the Lord saved me, I saw that I didn't need expensive things, so I used the money that I had saved to buy a good horse, although not a Pinto, a secondhand saddle without the silver decorations, and here is my pistol." He held up his Bible, adding, "And it always hits the mark."

When Luis became a Christian, he began working for the

Lord immediately. Before buying his horse, Luis would walk a long way every Saturday to visit his pastor so that he could explain the Sunday school lesson in Aztec. Then Luis would return to his remote mountain home where he would hold a Sunday school. He was superintendent, secretary, and treasurer as well as teacher.

God called Luis to preach, and he became one of their finest, hardworking pastors with unusual initiative. When Daisy visited his church along with the Solteros, a delightful surprise awaited them. A beautiful new church building, larger than their old one, stood ready for dedication that day. They had built it entirely without requesting help from the mission. Luis was probably most pleased that they had been able to surprise his beloved "Jefe," Brother Soltero.

Juan, the policeman from Xilitla, was introduced to Daisy's American audiences. Brother Juan was an alcoholic in his village further up in the mountains before God changed his life. And what a change! He wanted everyone he knew to be converted also, so he passed out tracts and testified to all his neighbors. Some irate people had him put in jail in Xilitla, the county seat. After serving his sentence, he returned to witness as usual, and again his enemies had him sentenced to another jail term.

This time, the authorities told Juan that they knew he had not committed any crime and agreed to let him out of jail on one condition. "We need you," they said. "We will let you out of jail if you will be our policeman here. We cannot let you go back to your village to live." So Brother Juan became the policeman of Xilitla.

Wherever Juan went, he carried tracts and gospels to give out. If he found a man sitting on a park bench, he would ask him, "Can you read? I have a good book here, but I don't read. Would you read it to me? Just start anywhere you wish."

After reading a little, the man would ask, "Where did you get this book? Can you get me one like this?"

Brother Juan's answer was always the same. "Since I can't read, I'll give you the book. Please continue to read it." This was his way of sharing the story of Jesus with many people.

Sometimes when he gave his testimony, he quoted scripture. Skeptical listeners in the audience loved to challenge him since everyone knew he didn't read. With a little twinkle in his eye, he would give them the reference and ask them to look it up. They were always surprised to find that he did know the verses.

One Sunday, Daisy was visiting the church in Xilitla when

Brother Juan came bringing three convicts from the jail. He seated them on the front bench and then sat on the platform next to the pastor. When the altar call was given at the conclusion of the message, Brother Juan stood up and motioned for his prisoners to come forward. Of course, they had to obey. Brother Juan knelt in front of them and prayed for each one. Whether they were born again or not, they would never forget the jailor who prayed for them.

It was faithful pastors like Luis and laymen like Juan who were instrumental in the rapid growth of the church in Mexico during those years. And it was their stories that touched the hearts of people at home, moving them to become faithful partners in prayer and financial supporters of the work.

The happiest times of all for Daisy were the months spent in Mexico. During one of those "teaching and visiting" parts of the year, she and Flora Belle ministered in Valles and the Huasteca. Teaching the students was a thrill as always, but nothing could compare with riding horseback over the familiar trails to the mountain churches for the sheer romance of missions. They stayed in the homes of the Mexican pastors, many of whom were their students during school sessions, even when parsonages were small and conditions not ideal.

> *Our institute keeps us busy. We have 28 students besides 2 extra ones in English that I'm teaching. Seventeen are new.*
>
> *Last Sunday a week ago, we went to Temalacaco. They had 250 for Sunday school, then preaching. I expect over 300 Indians — a good service. When we left the highway to go up the mountains to Xilitla, we found huge trees broken off and uprooted from a wind storm they had in the morning. We had a good service in an Indian church 3 miles beyond. It rained hard and plenty of lightning. When we returned to Abiel's it was still raining and plenty of thunder, so Bro. Soltero decided not to come down.*
>
> *We had some night of it. Aurora, Flora Belle, Raquel and I slept crosswise of the bed, and we sunk in the middle — was not even room enough to scratch the fleas that bothered! The babies cried, but not at the same time — the pigs scratched their sides on the outside of one wall of the house.*

The years of going and coming from Mexico ended in the middle of 1945 with one last, extraordinary trip. Daisy and Flora Belle traveled together from Indianapolis to Valles for the annual conference (name changed from assembly to conference during those years). This was the year for the twenty-fifth anniversary celebration and the end of the five-year plan to double the work.

General church officials, missionaries, visitors from other denominations in Mexico, delegates and many laymen filled the beautiful new church in Valles to capacity. There was great rejoicing as reports were given, revealing that they had reached and exceeded their goals in every area. There were ten ordained, eighteen licensed, and twenty-eight local ministers; fifty-one organized churches, thiry-one regular preaching points and 3,136 members.

Another ambitious plan of advancement was launched during that conference. Seven workers, all products of the Bible school, with their families were chosen to open a new district in the state of Puebla, south of Mexico City. The conference was deeply moved as the seven couples along with thirteen children lined up across the platform for their formal commissioning.

Daisy smiled amidst her tears. Among the group was Paulina, one of her little girls from San Luis more than fourteen years before. She had become the wife of Eduardo Munoz, a Bible school graduate, assistant superintendent to Brother Soltero, and now appointed to lead the first Mexican missionaries.

After conference, Daisy and Flora Belle visited most of the mountain churches in the Huasteca. They had their one and only ever experience of its kind on one of those treacherous mountain trails. Flora Belle declared it would have made a good movie. They had ridden their animals several hours up steep mountain trails when they came to a smooth slab of stone. The trail was narrow with no place to go except over that smooth slanted rock. Flora Belle, first in line, and always game for an adventure, gave her horse the command to continue. As the horse began to slip, she frantically pulled her feet out of the stirrups and rolled free before he fell. They both got up, and she mounted the horse again and continued the journey.

Less than a minute later, Daisy's mule's front feet slipped out from under him, somersaulting Daisy out of her saddle head over heels in front of him. Daisy landed slightly uphill from the mule, and found herself seated upright looking him straight in the eye. When they discovered that no one was hurt, everyone burst into laughter at the sight of Daisy and mule staring into each others eyes in shocked amazement. It took several minutes to gain control of herself before Daisy could stand. The pastor who was traveling with them decided that it was best that they walk the rest of the way.

That was Daisy's last trip to Mexico until almost seventeen years later. When she and Flora Belle left Valles at the end of June to resume their deputation travels in the north, they had no idea what further missionary adventures God was preparing for them.

Chapter 11

Another New Assignment
Pioneering in Puerto Rico

Ye have not chosen me, but I have chosen you, and ordained you, that ye should go and bring forth fruit, and that your fruit should remain; that whatsoever ye shall ask of the Father in my name, he may give it you (John 15:16 KJV).

Missionary gypsies? Could there be such a thing? By the time Daisy and Flora Belle made their 1945 trip to Mexico, they were almost beginning to feel like gypsies. They had no certain dwelling place except their suitcases. Where was home? Indianapolis, San Diego, San Antonio, Valles?

For weeks before their last visit to Mexico, Daisy had a growing inner compulsion that they should bring all their things with them to Indianapolis from San Antonio. Deep inside, she was allowing God to loosen the ties with her beloved Mexicans and her cherished missionary co-workers. God was changing the call from Mexico to "where needed most."

Indianapolis, Ind.
June 15, 1945

Dearest Folks,

The headquarters here has bought a new building as you have no doubt seen by the Advocate, and this Foreign Missions Department is moving next week. Then Flora Belle and I will move here to live, at least for the present.

We brought all our things, excepting furniture, up here

91

*from San Antonio, our books, bedding, curios, etc., so we
will have plenty to fix it up nicely. This will only be temporary, but we will enjoy it while we can.*

Rumors about starting work in Puerto Rico had been floating
around the missionary office for weeks. General Secretary
Thomas discussed the possibility with Daisy and Flora Belle, and
suggested that they might be the ones assigned to spy out the
land. It sent the two to their knees to find out if this was really
what God had in store for them. Excitement began to build as
they waited for a final decision.

At last it was official. These two "successful" missionaries
from the Mexican work seemed to be the logical ones to pioneer
the new mission field. They spoke Spanish fluently and made
adjustments easily. Solteros recommended them highly as missionaries with a passion for souls, a keen sense of spiritual dis-
cernment, and love for people. They believed in training local
people to do the work of the church and to carry financial
responsibility from the beginning, two cornerstones of the
indigenous approach to missionary work.

Daisy longed to visit her Mama and Papa in California
before going, but that was out of the question. There would be
no time for that.

Dear Mama,

*I should be excited, I guess, but really feel like I'm going
in circles. There is so much to be done, and we are going to
be pushed to the very limit to get it done. Today, Bro.
Thomas told us that we are to leave for Puerto Rico for 2 or
3 months or perhaps longer. We are to leave 2 weeks from
today if we can get ready that soon. That means by train to
Miami and then by airplane. What do you think of that? I
always said that when I went up in one of **them things** I
wanted to go places.*
WILL WONDERS NEVER CEASE?!

Daisy and Flora Belle had enough experience to know that
they were not being sent on a vacation. The task assigned to
them was awesome. There would be thrills to enjoy and battles
to be fought, new things to see, and the age-old enemies of the
gospel to be faced. To begin with, Daisy and Flora Belle
squeezed every possible bit of delight out of their first airplane
trip.

We came to Miami by train from Indianapolis, then left by plane after midnight on a beautiful moonlight night. There were a few electric storms around. Small but spectacular. Our plane came over the entrance to Haiti which seemed like large open arms. Two large pillars of clouds in various pastel colors towered around us. We flew in between and around these as though in fairy land. It was gorgeous! Below us were fishing boats with sails well-filled with early morning breezes, sailing a beautiful blue sea.

After a brief stop in Port-au-Prince, we flew over the highlands across into the Dominican Republic and then on to Puerto Rico, skirting three-fourths of its northern shore to reach San Juan. What a beautiful island, and what a coastline. The mountains which almost reach the sea are cultivated in part, but much is still heavily wooded. What beauty!

After the first couple of days in a hotel, they found temporary housing in a Methodist girls' boarding school in the Santurce area of San Juan. They created four small rooms out of their one large room with curtains and filing cabinets as they had learned to do in Mexico. They cooked on an electric hot plate set on a packing box. Years of improvising and being happy with less than the ideal made it easy for them to adjust to their new situation.

The two intrepid missionaries wasted no time in beginning their exploration of the island. They crisscrossed the mountainous terrain by bus or hired car, traveling over paved roads lined with beautiful flamboyant trees and deep red hibiscus bushes. They soon discovered that although the road system traversed the island, there were thousands of homes on the mountainsides that could be reached only by hiking or on horseback. They even visited off-shore islands by sailboat. They learned all they could about Puerto Rico, its people and its history, and discovered where other denominations were working.

They were almost overwhelmed with the opportunities for ministry wherever they went. People were bound by centuries of religion and superstition without a personal knowledge of Jesus as Savior. And everywhere, people were in need of medical help.

The big question was where to start the church. They prayed earnestly that God would guide them to the right place. Their strategy was to begin in the capital city of San Juan or as near as possible. They looked at dozens of properties for sale, but found nothing within the budget the department had given them. Rental properties were almost nonexistent. They soon realized that they must find a neighborhood where people were receptive and where their limited resources would allow them to minister without building a church before they had a congregation.

They finally chose a seacoast coconut plantation at the edge of San Juan in which to begin house-to-house visitation. They felt divine confirmation of their choice when the first home they visited was opened to them for Bible studies and Sunday school. The first regular service was held there in December, four months after they arrived in Puerto Rico.

Two friends of their hostess from a densely populated community in Santurce known as "El Fanquito" or "Little Mud" were in that first service. The Holy Spirit had already prepared their hearts to hear the gospel, and before long, they were both converted. Don (Mr.) Luis and Dona (Mrs.) Maria were so thrilled with their newfound peace that they asked Daisy and Flora Belle to begin services in their home in Santurce. They set aside two of the upstairs rooms in the living quarters above their place of business for a church. The children could be seated in one room and adults in the other, and the preacher would stand in the doorway between them.

There was a capacity crowd for the very first service in January. In response to the altar call, with no altar nor room to move, eight people knelt at their chairs and prayed for forgiveness. Among them was nine-year-old Mini who became a very important part of Daisy's life during her Puerto Rico years.

Sunday school and two evening services were held each week in the "upper rooms" in Little Mud, Santurce. God continued to bless their work with converts, and a church was born. By May 1946, Daisy reported to their friends at home that there were eight people who gave clear testimonies to being saved, and two other Sunday schools and Bible studies were being held each week. The great challenge was to find land on which a church might be built, or an existing building suitable for services. They started taking offerings, and challenged their people to pray and believe that God would provide what they needed.

Just as God was answering their prayers for a larger hall, it happened again! Flora Belle was desperately needed back in the States to do deputation.

For days, the two missionaries went about their work with heavy hearts not telling the church folks what was coming. How could she leave, when their new babes in Christ were growing, and so many more were near the kingdom? They had just begun to have Bible school classes three nights a week with one young couple who had been saved and called to the ministry. Several other young people professed a call and were eager to start classes. There were already more calls for Bible studies and Sunday schools than they could take care of.

The home office promised to send a couple to help with the work as soon as possible, and Flora Belle dutifully packed her suitcase and went back to Indianapolis, home base for deputation. Daisy agonized over the responsibility left to her.

> *When Flora Belle was called north, I felt as though the world had fallen on my shoulders. It seemed more than I could do here, and to be left alone has about floored me. But I marvel at how God has used the simplest of messages and given precious souls.*
>
> *Last Tuesday evening in testimony meeting, a young lady who has been saved just a few weeks said, after thanking the Lord for saving her, "I want to be sanctified, too, in order to be more secure." I gave an altar call at the end of the service and she came forward. Their faith is so simple. It is quite interesting to note that when they come to be saved we have to pray and they repeat what we say. But when they come for holiness, they do their own praying.*

Within two weeks after Flora Belle left, the little congregation moved out of the "upper rooms" into a much better place for worship. Don Luis vacated a part of his business quarters downstairs at the front of the building and made them into a church. The congregation paid him $15.00 a month rent, prepared benches and an altar, and even bought a piano. Seventy-three people attended the first service in their new church, July 14, 1946.

Two months later, Don Luis and Dona Maria built themselves another place at the back of the lot and allowed Daisy to have the entire upstairs for living quarters for a small additional rent. The church people were delighted to have her living among them. But Daisy was so busy that she asked God to send her help right away.

Daisy experienced another of God's unpredictable answers to prayer. One day, a tall, impressive Puerto Rican gentleman came to the door of the church. He asked many questions about the doctrines and practices of this new church that had appeared in the neighborhood. The sign above the door of the modest hall attracted him as he walked the streets of Little Mud performing his duties as a detective for the government.

Jose Molina had been raised in the old Methodist tradition and had studied for the ministry. Since leaving his home in the coastal city of Ponce and coming to San Juan to work, he had not been able to find a church that preached the doctrines of the church as he believed them. He drifted away from his moorings, but was hungry to be back in fellowship with the Lord and His people. As he listened to Daisy explain what the Pilgrim Holiness Church believed, he knew in his heart that this was what he was looking for. He began attending immediately and renewed his walk with the Lord.

His wife, Gloria, was reluctant to attend with him at first. During the course of her education at a university in New York, she had become disillusioned with her Catholic Church and decided not to attend church anywhere. She declared she could be a Christian and worship God without going to church. Upon returning to Puerto Rico, she married Jose and began teaching English in the city high school.

God used English-speaking Daisy's gentle ways, her winsome smile, and her American cooking to break down the barriers Gloria had put up. After a short time, Gloria joined her husband in the new church, a radiant Christian testifying in her vivacious manner to a completely new life in Jesus. Jose often preached and led Bible studies, and his wife helped with the children's work and played her saxophone for the services. Daisy divided the responsibilities for Bible studies and Sunday schools between her student couple, the Molinas, and herself.

As the weeks passed, Daisy felt that it would be better for Gonzalo and Monin to be in the Mexican Bible school where they would be in class with others. After much prayer God provided the means and she sent them and their two little sons to Valles into the care of the Solteros. Mini, Monin's nine-year-old sister who was living with them, found a home with Daisy. As the weeks passed by, several other young people felt called, and she knew from her experience in Mexico that soon they would have to start a Bible school of their own if the work was to prosper. The Molinas were ready to help her.

Almost a year after Daisy and Flora Belle arrived in Puerto Rico, she wrote home to her parents. Her letter was prophetic.

Two weeks from yesterday we will have been here a year. Wonder where I'll be next year! Perhaps I could easily wonder where I'll be next month. At least there isn't anything monotonous about my life!

In the midst of her busy life, a letter from Flora Belle came bringing a hint of a possible change. A holiness church in California was joining with the Pilgrims. Their missionary work in Israel and Peru was to be taken over by the missionary department. Finally, a letter came from the Reverend R. G. Flexon, the secretary of foreign missions who succeeded Paul Thomas. He told her that the General Board had voted to send the Gilmores from St. Croix, and that she would be sent to Peru to work with Flora Belle. They were being assigned to take over the Bible school. Daisy calculated that it would be at least a year before everything could be in place for that to happen.

But surprises continued to come. She was instructed to prepare to join Flora Belle by the middle of February in Florida. From there, they would fly together to Chiclayo, Peru. Even from the beginning of her time in Puerto Rico, she knew she would not be there permanently, but she found it difficult to leave these baby Christians. The hardest part of the plan, however, was having to forfeit a trip home to see her aging parents before going to Peru.

Daisy kept the news to herself for several days, feeling a need for confirmation from the Lord that this was His will. As she pondered the situation, she began to see that God was far ahead of her in His planning. The Gilmores had visited Puerto Rico twice during the past year, so the people already knew and loved them. She could see, too, that God knew all about this move when he brought Jose Molina to her door. Jose would be a wonderful help to the Gilmores in the work. Gloria would be an excellent Spanish teacher for them, far better than she.

The church was organized on her last Sunday in Puerto Rico with twenty-four members. That evening, they gave her a beautiful farewell service planned by Jose and Gloria Molina. They presented her with a Spanish Bible along with pictures of the Sunday school and the prospective student workers.

She would never forget the presentation speech. "In a war a general doesn't decorate his soldiers for each battle won, but presents them with a new sword to commemorate that battle and to prepare them for a new one. So we are giving you the Sword of the Spirit in memory of the battle won in Puerto Rico, and in preparation for the new battle in Peru."

Smiling through her tears, Daisy gave her challenge to her baby church. "All this time, I have been pointing you to Jesus. You have not been tied to me, but to Him. Please be faithful to Him no matter who is with you as your missionaries or pastors. If I never see you here again, I want to meet you all in heaven."

The next day, the new missionaries and a group from her church "family" watched as her plane lifted off and disappeared into the blue Caribbean sky. Daisy was on her way to Miami to meet Flora Belle and to finalize her visa to Peru. Once again, she surrendered her dream of visiting her family in California to the call of the missionary department. She didn't know then that it would be three more years before she would see them.

Chapter 12

Yet Another New Assignment

To the Land of the Incas

*Fear thou not; for I am with thee; be not dismayed;
. . . Behold, I will make thee a new sharp threshing instrument having teeth; thou shalt thresh the mountains, and
beat them small, and shalt make the hills as chaff . . . I will
open rivers in high places, and fountains in the midst of the
valley; I will make the wilderness a pool of water, and the
dry land springs of water (Isaiah 41:10,15,18 KJV).*

Destination, Chiclayo, Peru! Daisy and Flora Belle looked
forward to their new assignment with a mixture of excitement and reluctance. They revelled in travel like two
explorers setting out on untrod paths in search of hidden trea-
sure. Their small sense of reluctance to take over someone else's
work was completely overcome by the challenge of their new
assignment.

This time they were bound for the home of the Incas and
Quechuas — fascinating, ancient peoples whose cultures formed
the foundation of modern Peru. They discovered that three
Perus exist in this land of forbidding geography; the arid coast,
the frigid mountains, and the steaming jungle.

The Andes Mountains, towering to dizzying snow-capped
heights of almost 20,000 feet, zigzag their way through the
length of the land from north to south. They drop off abruptly
on the western side to a narrow rim of dry, sandy soil along the
Pacific Ocean cooled by the Humbolt Current sweeping up from
the Antartic. On the other side, the mountains suddenly plunge
down from lofty heights to the tropical jungles where isolated
tribes of primitive Indians live.

Daisy and Flora Belle watched eagerly for the first glimpse of their new home as their plane swept down over the mountains toward the setting sun and Chiclayo. They saw a city of flat-roofed adobe houses built on what appeared to be endless reaches of sand, with trees and flowers growing only where they could be watered by irrigation. The narrow cobblestone streets radiated from the harbor out across the sand dunes toward the lower slopes of the mountains. The surrounding countryside was barren and dry with vegetation and cultivated fields along the irrigation canals which brought water down from the mountains.

This city, which reminded Daisy of San Luis Potosi, was the center of the missionary work which the Pilgrim Holiness Church was taking over. The church and Bible school "plantel" (compound) near the heart of the city would be home for Daisy and Flora Belle. They found it to be a confined area containing a church, school building, dormitories, kitchen and dining room, and a small mission home all built of adobe brick plastered over with cement.

The buildings backed up to the perimeter of the property forming portions of the high wall which enclosed them. The spaces between buildings formed irregularly shaped patios where the students sat to chat or laundry flapped in the ever-present breeze. The only bits of green were found in a few potted plants or a patch of weeds and grass surrounding the laundry area or a water faucet. The two new missionaries were assigned an apartment in one of the buildings.

Daisy and Flora Belle needed very little time for making adjustments or dealing with culture shock, for this was Latin America. The people reminded them of Mexicans, and when the dust swirled around them with every small breeze, they looked at each other and said, "Just like San Ignacio." Outside of a few vocabulary modifications to accommodate Peruvian cultural differences, their Spanish was fluent and natural. It didn't take long to become acquainted with their new "family" and to understand what needed to be done.

Since their assignment was to take charge of the Bible Institute, they immediately began to ask questions about how the school was operated. They found that some aspects of the day-to-day operation would be retained by the missionaries of the group which had started the work. Daisy and Flora Belle were told they would teach, preach in chapel when asked, and become acquainted with the work in general by visiting the churches. That meant plunging immediately into preparations for school to start two weeks after they arrived. There were fifteen students, seven girls and eight young men.

Both Daisy and Flora Belle taught four hours of Bible subjects each day as well as music lessons to six students. In addition, Daisy taught Spanish four times a week to Leila Barton, their new young missionary co-worker who was sent by the former mission. Every Thursday evening was given to a Sunday school teacher training class. Later, Daisy also taught a nursing class once a week.

Weekends were spent visiting churches. Some were located in the mountain district with centers in Santiago de Chuco and Huamachuco, southeast of Chiclayo. Others were located in the coastal area around Chiclayo or a hundred miles to the south around the city of Trujillo. These were rewarding experiences affording them opportunities to get to know the character of the work. Most thrilling of all — they were able to contact many young people whom they challenged for the ministry.

Their work was not always easy. Sometimes frustrations with conflicting mission philosophy and ministry styles threatened to undo their peace of mind. Daisy wrote carefully about their problems to Mr. Flexon.

> *Have you heard about the volcano erupting here — it goes by the name, Slater! It is so far confined to our room, but surely God has given us this opportunity to preach the gospel here in the land of the Incas, and will give us the hearts of the people. Even that will take time. However neither of us feels like leaving, and though the battle may be a hard one, we know that God and our leaders are behind us.*

After the first few months, life settled into a routine of sorts — Bible Institute sessions alternating with visits to district centers for laymen's institutes or evangelistic services. Daisy could almost think she was back in the Huasteca in Mexico when she was in the mountains of Peru, except for the weather and the food. She never went anywhere without her medical equipment and bag of medicines.

> *From Trujillo to Huamachuco where I went is 110 miles and took 10 hours. The road is a good gravel mountain road with plenty of curves and plenty of steep grades. Part of the mountains we crossed were very high and barren, and we passed through a sleet storm both ways — something around 18,000 feet above sea level.*
>
> *After a convention in Huamachuco, we visited four con-*

*gregations and a few families in eight days. We were 56
hours on the trail. I went mule back most of the way. We
were 13 hours on the trail one day.*

*You should have seen me! With part wool underwear,
outing flannel bloomers that came over my knees, a pair of
cotton stockings and wool ones over them, my high top
boots, a slip, a dress, a sweater (all wool), my heavy navy
coat, a cotton head gear, a wool one over that, a hat on top
of that, and my dark glasses on.*

*We wear all the clothes we can to keep warm, and right
now, my feet are like ice. Flora Belle says she now knows
why these Indians worshipped the sun!*

*Did I tell you that I've eaten guinea pigs here? They are
much larger than those I saw in the States, and some are
beautiful — such lovely fur. They are good eating, too.
Most every home has them, and they live in the kitchen and
eat alfalfa.*

Daisy and Flora Belle developed a style of ministry in Peru
which was to mark their missionary careers from that time on.
The loving, selfless attention they gave their students, the discipline in daily living as well as the complete giving of themselves
to their physical and spiritual needs earned both of them the
title of "Mama." Their students and the young people in the
churches all poured out their problems and hurts to these two
who never seemed to run out of love and understanding.

When not in the classroom, the two Mamas could often be
seen supervising various campus projects, laughing and working
along with their children. Mama Florita ran out of energy
before Mama Daisy, and often had to spend time in bed.
Neither of them could figure out why she was so listless.

The school dining room became a cheerful, bright place with
new paint on the walls, compliments of Mama and Papa Buby.
Daisy made crisp white curtains for the windows and new tablecloths for the tables. She thought the project was not complete
without new dishes and glasses which she bought with her own
money. The happy chatter at mealtime, and the grateful thanks
of the students were her reward. Flora Belle accused her of trying to buy the love of the students, but she protested that she
felt they needed to have a morale booster. Gradually, the dormitory rooms and classrooms and library were brightened with
paint provided by the missionary department.

The boys took special delight in helping their Mamas to fix
up their own apartment with new paint and partitions to create

a guest bedroom which doubled as the school infirmary.

> *The rooms we're fixing for living room and guest room we've had a terrible time trying to get painted. First we tried lime then calcimine, then caseinite, and then gave up the job and washed all the several coats of "whatever" off. So now we're going to put on an oil paint. Later: the paint looks fine!*
>
> *Flora Belle is sick. Her blood pressure today is below 100 and she has no pep at all. It seems that the work is heavier every day and no sign of a let-up.*

The students loved to come into this "home" for long chats, to listen to records, or just to sit and read. It became a haven from their bustling school life and weekend ministries.

The names of their "children" began to appear in Daisy's letters to family and friends — Felix, Nato, Lucho, Juan, Julia, Gerardo, Francisco, Victor. One was an orphan with a gift for preaching who was sanctified in their living room one evening. Another was the only Christian in his family, the son of a school teacher, too young to be in the Bible Institute at first, but very gifted. Their discerning eyes could see tremendous potential for ministry in each one, reason enough to give extra attention in order to help them overcome all sorts of hindrances.

Leila Barton, a gifted pianist, became increasingly helpful in the school as she learned Spanish and Peruvian ways. She took the place of co-worker as well as daughter, calling Daisy and Flora Belle, Mama, like their Peruvian children. Some of the pastors, graduates of the Bible school were recruited to teach classes from time to time. Another of their faithful Peruvian helpers, Rebecca de Rojas, was the wife of the Chiclayo pastor. Her presence on the campus was invaluable whether teaching a class, or managing the marketing and the kitchen. She was their strong ally offering wise counsel and encouragement when the going was difficult.

The two "Mamas" delighted in giving special treats to their "family." Among them were trips to the simple mission beach house only a half hour's drive away from Chiclayo in the mission jeep. During school breaks, everyone looked forward to getting away from their cramped quarters to the open beach with the wide Pacific Ocean stretching out into infinity. Pent up tensions were released and horizons expanded as Flora Belle and some of the students romped in the breakers, while Mama Daisy and others watched from the safety of the sandy shore or set up a picnic lunch.

All the while, the students were prayed for and watched over as these two missionaries poured spiritual truths into them. Their goal was to see each student develop Christian character while learning theology and Bible and practical how-to's of the ministry. Most of their students came with only an elementary education and very little discipline except what was provided by the rigors and privations of life. They found the demands of keeping regular schedules for meals, classes, devotions, and studies difficult. Daisy and Flora Belle knew that the future of the work depended upon the faithfulness of disciplined pastors, and their responsibility to produce them was serious and demanding.

After their first graduation was held in December of their first year in Peru, a series of special meetings at the school including conference, kept everyone busy. It was almost time to prepare for the new school year when Daisy wrote home to her folks about her nursing activities.

> *It's been nearly 2 weeks since I wrote last — and what weeks! I guess I told you about Flora Belle. She has an ulcer. She's been quite miserable with her nerves and so weak at times and has spent the most of the time in bed. I'm giving her hypos every day, and she's on a diet with several meals extra per day. If she doesn't improve under this she'll have to go to Lima to see a specialist.*
>
> *Our boy, Lucho, went to Lima with his father. They found that his heart isn't so organically bad, but that he has T.B. and quite bad. He has to go to bed for a year. He has been in bed (at our house) the most of two days now, and seems to be resting. We are allowing him an hour at the piano every day. He has lots of music in him.*
>
> *Juan isn't doing too well. His throat isn't good, but he is much better than he was.*

With Daisy's expert nursing care, both Lucho and Juan improved dramatically. Lucho was able to return to his own home, but continued to spend most of his time on campus learning all he could from his two mothers there. Flora Belle's health continued to be fragile finally necessitating a trip to Lima with Leila as companion. Even then, they were unable to diagnose the difficulty, and Daisy confessed to being stumped. With large doses of rest, Flora Belle was able to teach and take her turn at chapel, but the heavy responsibility of supervision of the school and plantel fell to Daisy.

Changes came in the missionary family after the General Board appointed Francisco Soltero field superintendent over all the Latin American work of the Pilgrim Holiness Church. In May 1948, Coleman and Rita Avery were transferred from the Virgin Islands to Peru, and a few months later the missionaries of the former church returned to the United States.

Francisco Soltero's visit to Peru in August that year gave the work a tremendous forward thrust. Coleman Avery, with Lucho as his interpreter and right-hand man, took Francisco to visit the mountain churches. Francisco's anointed holiness preaching ignited revival fires in many of the churches and became a model for the young student preachers. Many of them declared they had never heard preaching like that — fiery, direct, and culturally fitting. His wise counsel and direction at district conference and in the pastors' institute prepared the way for future victories organizationally and spiritually.

After the district conference, Daisy, Flora Belle, and Lucho were assigned to accompany Francisco Soltero to Lima where they showed him the historical marvels of the city. Their proposed trip to Cuzco, the ancient Inca ruins high in the Andes Mountains, was cancelled when Daisy landed in the hospital for unexpected major surgery.

> *Here I am in bed yet in the hospital. Doctor says I'm doing fine. I guess Flora Belle wrote you all about the operation. I didn't want to tell you about it when it seemed that it might be cancer. The doctor was afraid of it, but it isn't! Thank the Lord!*
>
> *On Saturday evening, the last of the conference, I had such aching of legs and hips for two hours I could hardly sit still at supper. The ache was relieved, and was almost completely gone before going to sleep for the night. Flora Belle insisted on my having an exam. So the day we arrived, I came here. Doctor said operation.*
>
> *The first thing after my operation (after all the visiting with Bro. Soltero) is Flora Belle telling me that it isn't cancer. They took the uterus which had several fibroid tumors in it. He also took tubes and ovaries — says that at my age, 48, I don't need them any more. They also took the appendix. So I should be all fixed up for a long time.*
>
> *Bro. Soltero left last Tuesday. He said that he planned to stay until I either died or got out of danger, so why stay any longer! He went to Colombia and then on to Mexico. It*

sure was wonderful to have him here in Peru and especially here in Lima at this time. Brother Soltero, however, said that he wouldn't forgive me for robbing him of his trip to Cuzco! He is quite a tease.

The next months were spent at the beach house near Chiclayo recuperating. After a few weeks, Daisy went back into town to prepare for the opening of school the first of February 1949, and Flora Belle grew weaker. Doctors, baffled and unable to make a diagnosis other than extreme fatigue, ordered her to take a complete rest. That meant that Daisy supervised the Bible Institute alone and worried about her dear friend at the beach house. In addition to her duties as director and teacher, she had numerous responsibilities besides the school.

Am terribly behind on my account books. I'm local church secretary. That book is up to date. Also district secretary, and that's behind. Then I have a book for the school accounts and another for Flora Belle and me. They are both back — but maybe I can get at them soon. I should be triplets!

And then came the rains! The first since they arrived in Peru. They wreaked havoc on the adobe walls and roofs of their buildings. Water soaked through and ruined their lovely new paint, furniture, and many of their personal belongings. The disappointment was hard to take, especially when funds were scarce and repairs would be hard to make. Coleman Avery said the only comfort was that the whole of Chiclayo was in the same condition.

You should see our place. All of the roofs leaked. They are made of bamboo laid across the ceiling beams and mudded on top with a cement covering which was thin and cracked. Underneath was a mud plaster covered with white plaster. A lot of this has fallen! The chapel is the worst, but plaster has fallen in 11 different rooms. The ceilings are high and the noise of each fall has wakened us. People don't build here for any rainy season.

That school year, Daisy faced two painful disappointments which she handled with her characteristic "never give up" manner. Flora Belle was ordered home by her doctor because of her deteriorating health, and two of her "sons" at the school were conscripted into military service.

With all the love and consideration of her heart, she helped Flora Belle to prepare to go home. When life was at stake, Daisy had learned not to argue with the doctor. It was hard to put her on the boat in Lima, but Daisy did it with a smile and words of encouragement. After all, Daisy had already learned that it didn't pay to rebel against hard realities, or to pity herself when left alone. One of her favorite expressions was, "The Lord knows best." It helped to ease the loneliness to have Leila to move into Flora Belle's room.

But what about her two "sons" at the air base? In the past the church had lost some of its prime candidates for the ministry when they were called from the school into military service. Mama Daisy was determined that her students would not be added to the dropout statistics. She kept in constant touch with her "sons" through letters and frequent visits.

> *Our boys at the air base are doing fine. I went to see them yesterday, and they are radiant because of the way the Lord has helped them. They had to go to a dance, but when the officer called Presbiterio out to dance an Indian dance, he went to the officer and told him, "I'm an Evangelical (Protestant). I don't need these things to give me joy. I'm only here at the dance because I was ordered to come, but I cannot dance."*
>
> *The officer tried to intimidate him by ordering him to get on top of a wardrobe and pray to prove he was a Christian, and Presby said, "Very well," and climbed up. He took advantage of the opportunity and said a few words about the importance of being a Christian and what it involves and then prayed for them.*
>
> *The officer was much moved and said, "This young soldier has surely proved that he is an Evangelical, and I cannot make him do a thing against his conscience. I wish you were all like him."*

Word came from Flora Belle that extensive testing had revealed five kinds of parasites, some of which could have eventually taken her life. She was certain that with proper medication and rest, she would soon be back in Peru with Daisy. But it was not to be.

Daisy was called upon to complete that second school year and even to go through a third one in Chiclayo without Flora Belle. She wrote frequently about her students, many of whom became faithful workers in the church. Among them was their "son," Lucho, who continued to study and develop into an outstanding preacher and leader. What had been a brother/sister relationship between him and Leila blossomed into romance, and they planned to be married as soon as Lucho finished his school.

Between school terms, Daisy took helpers and traveled to some of the new churches which were being planted, places like Bambamarca, Cajamarca, and Cochicadan. As always, she taught and preached, and took care of the sick. Under the energetic leadership of Coleman Avery, the work was growing almost too fast to allow for thorough discipling of the new converts.

During that third school year, letters from home told of the trials of her aging parents. Her father became ill with a heart ailment, and her mother fell and broke her hip, requiring surgery. Elva, her sister, began to write about how much Papa and Mama longed to see her, suggesting that she ought to ask permission to go home.

As they moved toward the end of classes, Lucho and Leila set their wedding day, and Daisy began to talk and write about going home. It had been more than five years since she had seen her family, and it did seem that she ought to have a furlough. A letter from Flora Belle saying that the doctor would not release her for another whole year added to her sense of urgency that she should take some time off.

As always, when duty and privilege seemed to collide, Daisy struggled to reconcile the two. Added to the confusion were waves of homesickness rolling over her when she contemplated leaving her children, especially Lucho and Leila before their wedding. But as she prayed, she felt released from the school and became certain that she should go home.

Dearest Folks,

Yesterday I received such a happy letter from Elva Jane in which she says that you've had a letter from Bro. Flexon promising that I can go home at once. He wrote me, too. He was to have arrived in Mexico the 14th or 15th and was going to talk over plans with Bro. Soltero. So I should hear from them within the next week with definite plans.

It looks now as though I will get to leave for home sometime after June 4th. Just don't get your hopes up too far for a certain date. I expect it won't be past the middle of June anyway.

Daisy left all her belongings in Peru, absolutely certain that she would return to her family after a year accompanied by Flora Belle. She had no way of knowing that there would be a long interlude of thirteen years before she would see her Peruvian home again.

Chapter 13

Submission

Puerto Rico Again

*". . . I will come to you and fulfill my gracious promise
to bring you back to this place. For I know the plans I have
for you," declares the Lord, "plans to prosper you and not to
harm you, plans to give you hope and a future" Jeremiah
29:10b-11 (NIV).*

*H*ome again! But this time it was different. Flora Belle
helped to welcome Daisy to the Buby home which had
been moved to Spring Valley from San Diego. Papa and
several other members of her family made it seem like home,
but it wasn't quite right without Mama. She was in the hospital
barely hanging onto life, encouraged by Flora Belle who had
come early to keep reminding her that Daisy was really going to
be there soon.

After a few days, Daisy wrote to Mr. Flexon about her arrival
home.

> *My family sent two cables, and after the second it
> seemed imperative that I come. And since you had written
> both them and me that you would arrange for me to go
> home immediately, I took you at your word. Bro. Avery
> offered to take the school work to the end of this school year.*
>
> *When my mother saw me she cried and said, "My heart
> is about to burst!" We have had several good visits. She is
> begging the Lord to take her home soon.*
>
> *After a while, I believe I will be able to help out in some
> meetings, and then, please, I want to return to Peru in
> December if possible.*

Mr. Flexon's response to her letter made Daisy both happy
and a little apprehensive.

I am certainly glad that your mother is improving. I trust that she will be fully restored to her health and strength.

We want you to take off the entire summer for rest, with the exception of the missionary service at the El Monte camp. We do not have anything else booked for you until the fall.

You write about returning to Peru in December. These missionaries are strange people!! Don't you think you had better get your suitcase unpacked from your trip home before you begin to talk about your return??

Added to the joy of being with Mama and Papa and brothers and sister again was the excitement of seeing nieces and nephews, some grown into young adulthood since she had seen them last. She luxuriated in the comforts of home. What could compare with the convenience of drinking water without the process of boiling it, or a soothing hot bath straight from the faucet, or flipping a switch and always having light? She had almost forgotten how convenient and comfortable life in the United States could be. And then there were the visits of friends of other years and the wonderful music and preaching in the churches to make her heart overflow with joy. It was so good to be home!

Daisy's homecoming was an indescribable blessing for Mama and Papa Buby, too. Daisy did all she could to make life happier for her father who felt keenly the absence of his Bessie from their home. It was so good to have Daisy there to fuss over him and to have her reassurance about his physical problems. She kept both parents encouraged with the thought that soon Mama would be able to come home again.

Eventually, the letter came containing her schedule of deputation services for the fall, and once again, Daisy packed her suitcase with her speaking clothes and boarded the train for the east. During the fall months, her two requests from the department were that she be allowed to go home for Christmas since she had not been with any of her family during the holidays for 18 years, and the other was that she be allowed to return to Peru soon after.

Her first request was honored with no hesitation, but the second request was put on hold. In fact, the saga of "where to send Daisy" unfolded with hints of first one place and then another. Puerto Rico surfaced before Christmas as the most likely, with Daisy trying to reconcile the idea with her inner feeling that she really belonged in Peru along with Flora Belle. Her letter to her co-worker who was still recuperating back in California revealed her deep sense of disappointment at the prospect.

> *I don't know a thing more about Peru or Puerto Rico, but whether or not I'm to go to Puerto Rico, I surely don't feel like it. I find myself unconsciously planning all of the time for Peru. If the Lord wants me in Puerto Rico, the Lord would have to prepare me with an awfully big dose of grace. It wouldn't be easy, but I have put the case in the Lord's hands. It is true that Puerto Rico needs our help and that is our child, too.*

Before Christmas, it was settled that Daisy would go to Puerto Rico to take charge of the Bible school instead of returning to Peru, and she had to come to terms with the change. It was difficult, too, to accept the fact that Flora Belle could not go along — the doctor ordered continued treatment. She was not released to go anywhere for at least six more months. With that quiet resignation which so characterized this servant of the Lord and the church, Daisy made her way back to Indianapolis after Christmas to prepare for Puerto Rico.

Daisy came off the plane in San Juan in April 1951 to a jubilant welcome by her Puerto Rican family. It really was like coming home again, because almost everyone in the welcoming party had been converted while she was there the first time. She found that the fruit of her labors had remained! There were tears and hugs and joyous words of welcome, but the questions soon followed. "When will Flora Belle come? We need her here, too." She wrote about her conflicting emotions to her friends of the Round Robin.

> *You can imagine how disappointed I was not to be able to return to my Peruvian family. I'm sure it was the hardest thing that I'd been asked to do. My only consolation has been from the Lord. I have learned that when He takes away one thing He gives better in its place. Of course, I loved these Puerto Ricans, because Flora Belle and I had the privilege of opening the work here. It looks as though as badly as I felt the Peruvian work needed help that this has needed it more, though in a different way. I do not know how long I will be here, but I feel that the Lord is going to permit me to return to Peru some day.*

Even though many things had remained the same during the four years since she left, there were changes. The Gilmores were gone and Andres and Rachel Vega from Mexico were carrying on the work. It "helped" (one of Daisy's favorite expressions) that she knew Andres and Rachel well — Andres had been her student years before in Mexico Bible School days. Rachel was the niece of Francisco Soltero who went from Colorado to teach, and when Andres finished his school, he married his beautiful, vivacious teacher.

For her second term of service in Puerto Rico, she was welcomed to a lovely new Bible school property and comfortable home. She described it for her friends.

We have a beautiful property here, and so quiet. A big lawn, nice shade and fruit trees, some flowers and room for more, and room for a nice garden. The Vegas have a lovely 3-room apartment over the triple garage. I have the big house. It is 32x50 and has a large screened front porch 10x32 with a side porch attached where we do most of our living.

A few months after her arrival, a letter came from Flora Belle which ended the dream of their working together again. It completely revolutionized Daisy's thinking about herself and her ministry.

Your letter telling me about plans to send you to Mindanao (Philippines) has left me stunned! . . . All I can say is that if you and I are needed in two places instead of together, the Lord will help us to be the blessing that we should be. And after all, this is only for time. Eternity will be different — far different than we realize. It wasn't so hard expecting you to come some time in the near future.

One thing that I feel is as though the props had been removed. Perhaps I needed just that, but it seemed as though — and does yet — that you can teach so much better and clearer than I. And I was depending upon you to come and help make things clear to the class. Now I must depend upon the Lord to help me do what I expected Him to help you to do!

It would be 19 years before these two missionary ladies would be able to work together again. Flora Belle went to the Philippines in October of that same year and served until retirement and even beyond. There would be many more unexpected turns and detours in Daisy's path before her "afterglow" years.

God proved himself to Daisy and the work in Puerto Rico in miraculous ways during the next two years. Only a few months after that soul-shaking letter, God turned what seemed to be a severe disruption of the work in Santurce into a blessing. The government's decision to build a highway through the area threatened to close the work.

The strip of land designated for the project included Don Luis's which meant that there would be no more church. Don Luis and Dona Maria were forced to sell their entire property to the government. Not to be outdone, Don Luis searched diligently until he found another property suitable for a church in the same area, bought it, and made it into a church. Attendance increased even though some of the members were also dislocated and had to move too far away to continue to attend there. God turned the hindrances into blessings.

One of those was Don Moises who found work and a home in Catano, a town on the edge of the bay west of San Juan. He immediately called for help to start a church in his home for his neighbors. As people were saved, a congregation was formed and built their own small church. That congregation planted another daughter church in Maguayo, where the parents of Don Moises lived. Through the combined efforts of all three congregations, another small property was purchased and a church built. Within a few short months, what seemed to be a disaster for the young church actually proved to be God's way of multiplying it. Eventually, a congregation was formed in Ponce, the hometown of the Molinas.

Meanwhile, Daisy was hard at work with her Bible school which she had started almost immediately after her arrival. She had three day students, Eloy Figueroa, Ruben Torres, Pedro Torres, at the big house in Rio Piedras, two of them boarding. She also taught classes three nights a week in the Santurce Church, a half hour bus ride from the Bible school. There she had six students who could not study during the day because of family concerns.

Within a year, the Vegas returned to Mexico, and the Yoders, a new missionary couple from Pennsylvania took their place. The Yoders fit in beautifully immediately, having served in Honduras under another mission before coming to Puerto Rico. Mini came once again to live with Daisy and to take special classes designed especially for her.

The small congregations continued to grow and reach out.

It took the combined efforts of Daisy, the Yoders, and the ministerial students to carry on the four churches and a new outreach
in a town some distance from San Juan.

> *With the new place, it means that the Yoders will be in
> Santurce Sunday evening, Catano Tuesday evening,
> Maguayo Wednesday evening, Monin's home Thursday and
> Arecibo on Friday and Sunday a.m and afternoon. Pedro
> teaches Sunday School class Sunday a.m. in Santurce and
> has S.S. in Maguayo in the afternoon and preaching there in
> the evening. He will take the Friday evening service in
> Catano. I take the evening service in Catano on Sunday
> with Mini. Both of us teach a S.S. class in Santurce in the
> a.m. and in Arecibo in the afternoon, and I have Bible study
> in Santurce on Tuesday evening. And besides that, we are
> having classes.*
>
> *Sundays we are in the car a total of 5 hours going and
> coming to services, and that makes us all pretty tired to start
> the week. But there is such good interest in our new place
> that we don't want to stop.*

By the time Daisy left again for deputation in mid-1953, the
work was progressing rapidly with three of their congregations
worshiping in new church buildings. Besides these there were
several preaching points and Bible studies each week.

Pedro Torres, one of her most promising students, finished
the three-year ministerial course and was graduated one day and
married to Mini the next. Daisy spent many hours of her last
few weeks helping this couple, both without parents, to prepare
for their wedding. With great satisfaction, she was able to see
them take their place in Catano as the first full-time Puerto
Rican pastoral couple. It was a fitting conclusion for her Puerto
Rico years.

As usual, Daisy was handed a full schedule of deputation
meetings for the summer and fall months upon her arrival in
Indianapolis. When she was in the city, she lived in her room at
the old headquarters-turned-mission-home. She and Flora Belle
had left some of their belongings there to be used by whichever
would need them. It was wonderful to share experiences with
other furloughing missionaries, but she found it difficult to keep
Papa and Mama surrendered to the Lord. They were all living
for the holiday season when she would be home again.

Sometimes she wished she was not so close to the office. Mr.
Flexon had too many ideas about where she might serve next,

and all the while she was sure she should return to Peru. His first plan was for her to go to South Africa where a nurse was badly needed. If so, she would be required to take some nursing classes to update her knowledge and skills in preparation for this new assignment. Then came the holiday break at home, almost like a reprieve from some kind of heavy sentence which was about to be pronounced upon her. After she was back on the deputation trail again, she wrote about how wonderful it had been to be at home.

Jan. 3, 1954

Dearest Folks,

How are you this evening? It doesn't hardly seem possible that I was there day before yesterday. But, my! What a wonderful 6 weeks I had with you all! There are lots of things that I'd like to have done for you, but I guess I just didn't manage right. There were the curtains and the chair, and cleaning the house again, and. . . . and. . . . and. . . . Perhaps Elva Jane will be able to do some, and if not they will have to wait until my next trip.

It was so nice to have both of you at home. It seemed so much more "homey." Mama, you take care of Papa, and Papa, you see that Mama behaves herself.

And since I'm needed back here we will accept it as from the Lord, and expect Him to make a way for another good long visit.

She was back in the east again, resuming her deputation ministries and making plans for those nursing classes. Before she could begin on the project, a desperate call came from home. Her father was in critical condition with a serious case of shingles, and needed her. Mama was desperate for her to come, because she was helpless to cope with the situation, confined as she was to either her bed or the wheelchair designed and built especially for her by Papa. It wasn't enough that Elva Jane was near and willing to do anything she could. They wanted their nurse, so Daisy dropped everything and went.

The next two months for Daisy were filled with constant care of her Papa, and deep concern over her own future. Her heart was not at peace with the appointment to Africa, but she felt there was little she could do about it except to pray. Finally a letter came from Mr. Flexon, changing the plan.

*I have certainly not been clear in sending you to Africa,
and it seems that a number of our Executive Council members have been feeling the same way. So, after much discus-
sion and prayer the Executive Council feels that there is a
need for your services in our Bible School on the island of
Barbados. We hope to open this school next September with
about 20 students. . . .*

*I trust your father has improved and that you are enjoy-
ing your visit with your parents.*

Barbados? That was a completely new and different idea
which she needed to think and pray about again. How could it
possibly be? As she placed the matter before her Lord, He
impressed upon her a deep sense of responsibility to her parents.
Her father was improving from the shingles, but was far from
well. Her mother was an invalid whose broken hip had never
mended, causing intense suffering from time to time, requiring
constant nursing care. It seemed that for now, this was to be her
assignment from the Lord. She finally had the courage to write
the letter informing her leader about her decision. His response
was kind and understanding.

*I received your letter and was somewhat disappointed.
However, I can understand your position and feel that you
have made a proper decision, for I am sure that your parents
need you and you will never regret doing all that you possibly can for them while the Lord permits you to have them
with you.*

*We will grant you a leave of absence from the mission-
ary department for as long as you feel it necessary, but when
you are ready to take up work again with the department
there will be a place for you.*

If Daisy had known when she arrived back home in Spring
Valley on February 24, 1954, that she would be there for the
next nine years, she would have found the prospect devastating.
Mercifully, God kept the future to himself, and promised grace
sufficient for her days. Daisy was determined to live her life to
the full wherever she was, taking what God sent her way day by
day as from His gracious hand.

There were special events, some sad and some glad, sprinkled through the years at home. Some of her nieces and
nephews were married, and some of them entered the ministry.
Daisy was saddened by the homegoing of her schoolteacher

brother, Alvin, at the age of 52, but she was glad to be there to help ease the hurt for her parents. There were birthdays and wedding anniversaries for her parents celebrated lovingly by family and friends.

After several months of Daisy's expert nursing care, her father's health improved so much that he was once more able to work in his carpentry shop building pulpit furniture from fine wood for churches in the area. Mama's creative family found a way to take her to church and for occasional drives through the countryside.

> *Mother is about as usual, cheerful and quite comfortable. My brother Billy who is one of the managers at Douglas Aircraft in Tulsa, Oklahoma, was home for two weeks. He took us out for two nice rides and mother enjoyed that. We take the front seat out and use a chair for the driver's seat (fastened down). Then we roll Mom into the car on a ramp from the porch, thus making an ambulance out of the old Buick.*

Almost nine long years passed in the care of her parents, years of patient, loving, sacrificial giving of herself to their needs. At first, they were well enough for Elva to relieve her of the day-to-day responsibilities for a weekend now and then. These were times of rest and spiritual renewal at camp meetings and special services, or refreshing visits with her friends in Pasadena.

As time and medical crises took their toll on both parents, Daisy seldom left the house. Mama and Papa were finally confined to their hospital beds at home, Mama's in the living room. She rearranged the furniture so that Papa's bed could be rolled in from his room for some pleasant hours with her through the day. Bible reading, singing of hymns, and quiet visits from loved ones and friends kept the days from becoming one long blur of pain. Both parents remained cheerful and uncomplaining even when the days were the darkest, and Papa's dry wit gave Daisy lots of laughs.

Through all those years, letters to and from Flora Belle, the "Robins," and her missionary family in three countries helped to keep her world from shrinking inside the four walls of the little house in Spring Valley. The burden for a world in need of a Savior still motivated her praying and giving. At one point, she signed over all her Missionary Retirement Fund to the department to be divided between special needs in Mexico and Peru.

She never lost touch with what was going on in her larger family, nor was her vision for continued missionary service obliterated by the immediate demands upon her time and energy. She had given herself to God long ago to be his missionary servant, and she was certain the assignment in Spring Valley was not to be permanent.

Chapter 14

A Missionary Again

Back Home in Peru

The Lord is good to those whose hope is in him, to the one who seeks him; it is good to wait quietly for the salvation of the lord (Lamentations 3:25-26 NIV).

*H*eaven and earth came together in the little house in Spring Valley during the third week of October 1961. Mama Buby was nearing her eternal home, and her family waited for her crossing. During the last few weeks of her earthly journey, God seemed to beckon to her from heaven. Even though she did not respond to her family's attempts to communicate with her, occasionally her face would glow with a radiant smile as she looked beyond them into the distance and said, "The Lord has been so good to me," or "Yes, I'm ready to go." They knew she was talking to an unseen presence.

The day Mama went to heaven, Daisy prepared her father for the event and then wheeled his bed into the room with her mother. She called her sister from her home nearby, and together they had their usual family devotions. Ten minutes after they prayed, Mama went quietly, peacefully to be with the Lord.

Papa waited eight more months, often saying that he wanted the Lord to take him so that Daisy could go back to her missionary work. An hour before his death, Daisy left the room for a few moments. When she returned she was confronted with a worried question from Papa, "Where are you going?"

"Why, Papa, I'm not going anywhere as long as you need me," Daisy responded without a trace of annoyance in her voice.

This time, Papa had an announcement of his own to make. With his children and many of his grandchildren gathered around him, he looked up at Daisy with something of the old twinkle in his eye and declared confidently, "I'm going on a trip." William Buby began his earthly journey with his Lord in

1887 and completed it on June 4, 1962.

The realization finally dawned on Daisy that the long years of sacrificial service to her parents were over. She was released from the Lord's assignment in Spring Valley, and she knew exactly what to do next. She wrote to the missionary department announcing that her vigil over her parents had ended and that she was ready to return to Peru. The prompt response from the new secretary of world missions, the Reverend E. L. Wilson, sent her into a flurry of plans.

> *This is to inform you that the Executive Council has recommended to the General Board your appointment to the mission field. It must be ratified by the General Board in November. We are planning to send you to Peru for the Bible school work. The Rundells (new missionaries who had followed her) are coming home in December.*
>
> *Can we depend on you to be available to help us in the Self-Denial push in September, October, and November? Perhaps you could go to the field in December.*

Daisy's family insisted that before she obligated herself for missionary duties again, she must have a long-overdue vacation. It was arranged that she would travel with Billy and Mary, his wife, to Seattle, Washington, and back again. It almost seemed to her like a sin to take so much time just for enjoyment, but as the weeks of complete rest from responsibilities passed, she realized how much she needed that time for adjusting her mind and heart to life without her parents.

Only one thing happened to mar the nearly perfect vacation — the death of her brother, Nelson, who was suffering with heart problems even while her father was ill. Her family assured her that it was all right that she was not there when he joined Alvin, Mama, and Papa in heaven. It was hard to realize that in such a short time, four of seven members of her immediate family were gone, but her sense of loss was mixed with joy that all were with the Lord.

The months from July until the next February were filled with preparations for Peru and all the legal involvements of settling her parents' estate. Although she did not assist in the regular deputation schedule again, her visit back east to Indianapolis allowed her to become acquainted with new people in the world missions offices and to visit relatives in Michigan once again. On her way back to California she was thrilled with a visit to Mexico and San Ignacio.

> *Dear Martha is the same faithful cheerful stand-by. She and I went to San Luis Potosi and on to Valles together. There are still some of the folks in the San Luis church who were at my welcome service in July, 1928. There are some fine churches all over Mexico as a monument to Bro. and Sis. Soltero's faithful labors over the past 43 years.*
>
> *Martha and I had a wonderful trip to my old pastorate in San Ygnacio . . . did so enjoy the few minutes with many of our old friends as we visited in their homes.*
>
> *To date since my father went Home, I've traveled over 14,000 miles. The Lord has been so good to me. And now to go back to Peru!*

Daisy was amazed at the number of forms to fill out and requirements to meet before she would be cleared for missionary service again. How different it was when she went out by faith 35 years before, simply packing her trunks and suitcases, buying her ticket herself, and boarding the train! No one seemed to care whether she was in good health, or had a police record, or who gave her money. Now, she had to fill out an application for missionary service, have a physical exam and obtain medical clearance for the department of world missions, sign a contract, make six copies of the lists of every item in her freight including evaluations for customs and the freight company and the department, and more!

Besides all that, the Peruvian government required medical clearance, immunizations, authorization of her assignment in Peru, proof of her professional preparation, and a police clearance before they would grant a visa. To complicate matters, a coup in Peru threatened to prevent her going. The Peruvian self-installed military government countered the withdrawal of all United States aid from the country with stricter controls of their own on Americans wishing to enter. They even "lost" the first visa application.

Careful, cooperative Daisy completed the last requirements and made her plane reservations for February 18, with arrival in Lima on February 21.

> *My shots — smallpox, 3 typhoid, tetanus and yellow fever have all been taken. My physical exams taken, eyes tested and new lenses, teeth fixed, my ocean-going baggage on its way to arrive when I do. Now only last loose ends to gather up.*
>
> *What a tremendous responsibility before me! It won't be easy. I will need all the prayer backing I can get.*

Daisy's heart was almost bursting with joy as she arrived at the Bible school plantel in Chiclayo where she received a jubilant welcome. Not much had changed over the years, except for a different group of young people in the school and the dramatic growth in the district. Most of her students from more than a decade ago were now pastoring the churches and taking responsibility for the work in various parts of Peru.

She immediately became "Mama" again, but this time she was determined to be more professional in her approach to her work as principal of the school, and a little less emotional in her attachment to her students. And yet, tenderhearted Daisy found it impossible not to love those young people as she would have loved children of her own.

It was natural for the students to call her Mama out of respect for her white hair and her age — almost 63. She looked older, but her step was still lively and determined. Her keen mind, quick perception of what was going on around her, and efficient ways of managing the school commanded their respect and cooperation — most of the time.

One of her first-year students was a young woman who declared that she was called to the ministry. It didn't take Mama Daisy long to discern that she was really called to find a husband. It demanded all the patience and wisdom Daisy had to deal with her constant attempts to gain the attention of the young man she had chosen.

The situation afforded Daisy the opportunity to give instruction about the real purpose of attending the Bible Institute, and what constituted a "proper" courtship. She agreed that it was wonderful for young people who were called to the ministry to marry each other, but there were rules to be followed. Instilling biblical principals of chastity in her "children" was a challenge in a culture which tended to look the other way when young people made "mistakes." She insisted that their relationships be thoroughly Christian and carefully chaperoned.

There were seventeen students to teach and care for that first year. Keeping the electricity turned on and food on the table proved to be a challenge. Some support for the school came from the home office, some from the churches in the district, and some from Church World Service. Daisy taught her students to be frugal, a characteristic she had learned as a child. She never wasted anything, not even a bit of leftover food. It went into a container to be used in "leave-over" soup.

We go down to the fishing village once a week and

watch the fishing boats come in, and get enough fish for two or three meals. We have gotten tuna that weighs around 6 pounds for 12 cents. Two of them, stuffed and baked, make a tremendous meal for our students with leave-overs for soup. By the way, did you ever eat fish soup? Or better still, how about fish head (including the eyes) soup? Not a favorite of mine, but a delicacy here in Peru. I eat all my meals with the students. We are a happy family.

Besides teaching a full load of classes and managing the school, Daisy visited sixteen churches including a trip to the mountains within the first five months after she arrived. She discovered that those trips over rugged mountain roads by bus or truck were not as easy as when she was younger. Neither were the long hours spent in the saddle, but she was determined to be a cheerleader for her "children" who served in these remote places as well as their teacher.

Our convention was from Tuesday evening through the following Sunday. Day time was clear and so pretty. No smog there, but the minute the sun went down it was bitterly cold. We took blankets to church to wrap up in. The trip down was one never to be forgotten. The new bus had every seat taken with little stools for jump seats down the aisle and then people standing. On top there was a tremendous load of baggage and freight and 14 more passengers. On the crooked mountain roads we averaged about 8-10 miles per hour. It took us 10 hours to come 120 miles. Our driver was very careful for which I was especially glad.

Life for the next seven years fell into a rhythm of sorts — school terms of three months interspersed with conferences, lay workers institutes held in churches, and visits to the preaching points where her students were serving. She told the "Robins" about the closing of the school year and some of their vacation victories.

School closed December 6th, with three graduates. The young lady married one of our pastors and seems to be fitting in very well. Both of the young men went to the edge of the jungle to two different sections where they were calling for preachers. One went to La Peca where he found several Christians. He started the first Sunday school with 22 in attendance, dedicated 7 children and had 5 new converts that first Sunday. The other went to an entirely new section where he dug out three preaching points, and there are 35 converts as a result of his summer's work.

In January I spent a few days in Cutervo, high in the mountains. This is a lovely town with a good congregation. While there, I visited the home of one of my students which was an hour and 40 minutes by horseback, almost straight up the mountain. They treated me to the best that they had. There were 50 packed into the small room for service that night. The women with their babies were sitting on the floor, and only a few of the men had chairs.

They served me delicious meals prepared in the most primitive manner. I sat on a low, rickety chair at a low table with the guinea pigs running around at my feet. The stove was three rocks so situated on the dirt floor as to be able to balance the big clay pot. The roof is thatched, and the walls are bamboo poles with mud over part of them to keep out the wind. A swinging shelf in one corner held the necessities of life. The baby was swinging in a hammock, or tied on its mother's back. The mother and grandmother squatted by the fire to tend to the meal. The other members of the family sat on a log. The dogs and the pigs wanted to come in, too.

In spite of all of this, or maybe because of it, the chicken soup was delicious, after which they served rice with peas, and fried guinea pig with coffee and bread. There is a flavor to these meals that comes from their hospitality, and I don't even mind the smoke too much.

Mama Daisy's example of selfless service and concern for the salvation of the people around her was a constant inspiration to her students. When she assigned them to evangelistic work in hard places, everyone said, "If Mama can go there, we can too."

Even though Daisy's primary ministry was the Bible school, her medical knowledge and skills were put to use constantly. Sometimes there were babies to deliver for the wives of the pastors or married students. It seemed that her students also needed constant medical care for simple ailments such as headaches or flu, and sometimes for more serious ones. Once an epidemic of mumps swept through the school with eight of her young men down at the same time.

Daisy never gave up on the young people whom she felt were being called of God for the ministry, never wanting anyone to settle for God's second best. One of them was a gifted son of one of the pastors whose wife, Rebecca de Rojas, had worked with her in the Bible school all through the years. He tried to enroll in the University in Lima, and was plunged into deep despair when his application was turned down. Daisy felt all along that God was at work, preserving him for the ministry.

Mama Daisy went to work, too. She convinced him to go with her to the youth convention in the mountains during the holiday break from school, and paid his way. While there, he answered God's call to be a preacher of the gospel. Before the next term at the Bible school began, he turned down four job offers, fearing that he would be sidetracked from the call God had given. But when it came time to enroll, he had no money. Daisy took him into the school, prayed with him for the supply of his needs, and finally saw him graduate. He eventually became an outstanding preacher and church planter in Latin America.

The Peruvian Church experienced tremendous growth during the sixties, and Daisy's work in the Bible school was at the heart of it all. Opportunities for church planting and calls for pastors were coming from all over Peru. When Coleman Avery gave his report to the annual conference in 1966, he said, "The doors aren't just open, they are off their hinges."

That year, Daisy's secret worry was that the missionary leaders at home might insist that she leave the field because of her age. She wrote to Flora Belle in the Philippines.

> *I would like to stay through next year and then go for a year. In that way these new students could be out in their year of practicum while I am gone. I fear that they won't want me much longer. I'm 66 now. I don't want to give up any sooner than necessary.*

She really didn't need to be concerned. She was to be needed more desperately than ever before.

Francisco Soltero was present for their conference in 1967. By then, there were 37 organized churches and 63 preaching points. Nine new churches with 400 new members were added that year, and ten men and four ladies were ordained. Later during his visit, the one district was divided into three, each having its own Peruvian district superintendent and district council. A field council was formed, composed of the field superintendent, the missionary leader, each district superintendent, and a delegate from each district. The reorganization gave impetus to still further development and growth in the work.

Before long, Coleman Avery's health deteriorated rapidly requiring their withdrawal from the field. Daisy and Naomi Greer, her missionary co-worker who came from her outstation work to help Daisy with the teaching load at the school, were left to care for the work alone. She had confidence that the districts would continue to grow under Peruvian leadership, and they did.

At the beginning of the new school year in 1969, her last in Peru, Daisy wrote a glowing report of the activities of the pastors and her students to the home office.

A new school year has begun. What thrills there are in welcoming new students and hearing the interesting reports of those who spent their vacation in the work of the Lord. Almost everyone did!

There are 38 students this year, the third year in a row that we have broken the record. Besides these there are five in their year of practice which comes after their third year. We have three more who are attending a class or two a day from the city, and 19 first year students.

Almost two years ago one of our third year boys had to go into the army. The jolt was pretty hard for him, but he took the challenge and appointment as from the Lord. On his second day at the barracks he took an open stand for the Lord. Less that two weeks later his sargeant was definitely converted. The sargeant was discharged last year and is one of our new recruits here this year.

In the interior district, Felipe Vasquez is a pastor in an out-of-the-way village of Puentecillos. The congregation is large. Frequently some of the young men have to sit on the ceiling beams in order to be under the roof for service. They need a new church very much, but after buying a lot on the main plaza the authorities, backed by the priest, took Felipe to jail in the county seat.

The brethren went along with him, saying that they would not let him go alone. They sang all the way, about two hours on foot. At the jail a stranger took them a donkey load of blankets. A lady took their meals all prepared to them, since neither is supplied in the Peruvian jails. They said that they had a real fiesta instead of feeling like they were in prison. They sang, prayed, testified, and preached all the time that they were there. The next day they were sent home. They now have a permit to build with government backing.

A year ago, a man was sent from the mountains to the Federal prison near Lima. After leaving prison he went to our church in Comas, Lima, and was definitely saved. In August he attended the district young peoples convention, and wanting to tell his family how he had found God, he invited his pastor to accompany him on to Sihuas. They found many hungry hearts, and invitations for a pastor to come to minister to them. After graduation in December we sent one of the graduates with a fine first year student to work in that region.

Alvaro has returned to continue his studies and gives reports of having had over 90 converts in three months there. Eladio writes asking for special speakers for a series of meetings in August when they will dedicate the babies and baptize the new converts. He has three preaching points, and so many calls that he is unable to care for them all.

There are so many needy people. May the Lord help us!

Toward the end of the year, three new missionaries arrived. LaMar and Becky Brown with their infant son took up the responsibilities laid down by Averys. Miss Dorothy Brown, formerly having served in another Latin American country, came to help in the school. As the young missionaries made adjustments and became fluent in Spanish, Daisy began to have an inner sense that her time in Peru could be drawing to a close. One small comment in a letter to the "Robins" showed that she might be ready to stop. "Can't make it much longer — too heavy a load."

The visit of Daisy's sister and her husband, Elva Jane and Alvin Osborn gave her a bit of respite that year. Their testimonies and beautiful ministry through song and music (Elva was an accomplished keyboard artist) were like a lovely breath of fresh air from home. And of course, Daisy saw to it that they visited the historical and architectural wonders of Peru! Months later as Daisy looked back on their visit, she realized how God had given her one last tour of this country which she had come to love so much.

When school year closed at the end of October that year, Daisy felt released to go home for a short furlough. She wrote about her plans to her friends.

December 17, 1969

I arrived home (in Spring Valley) on November 3rd. Now my plans are, the Lord willing, to return to Peru the first of April for a new school year. Headquarters is making plans to send a new couple to take over the Bible school, but they will probably need a year in language school first. Then I will help to orient them, and then maybe I can start somewhere else!

The next several months were wonderfully satisfying for Daisy. Among other things, there were visits to headquarters in Indiana and to Billy's home in Tulsa, Oklahoma. A visit to Mexico for the fiftieth anniversary of the work filled her cup of joy to overflowing. It was a nostalgic journey back to the places where her missionary career began 42 years before.

March 16, 1970

Then the 50th anniversary in Mexico. What a wonderful time! We felt like building tabernacles there and staying on. . . . The Lord gave Bro. Soltero strength to go thru the whole thing. . . . And since the anniversary I have done deputation for three and a half weeks on this district (California).

And then came the bitter-sweet, surprise announcement!

Now, since they say that I'm to be retired, I'm planning on going to the Philippines in June. Flora Belle and I are planning on returning from there around the world.

When Daisy left Peru months before, she didn't know that those goodbyes would be final. It wasn't easy to commit her Peruvian family to the Lord without proper farewells, but she had done it once before, and she did it again. When she wrote asking for her belongings to be sent to her, it was like writing the last chapter on her missionary career — at least in Peru. She had to confess that at 70, she was happy to be free from responsibility, but she eagerly looked forward to the fulfillment of some of her other lifelong dreams.

That was Daisy's first retirement.

Part IV

The Rewarding Years
Afterglow

"Sooner or later, everyone sits down to a banquet of consequences."

Robert Louis Stevenson

Chapter 15

Retirement?
New Adventures

But the path of the just is as a shining light, that shineth more and more unto the perfect day (Proverbs 4:18 KJV).

Dreams really do come true! And God does keep His promises! Daisy's heart sang with joy as the big plane touched down at the Manila International Airport on a steamy summer day in June, 1970. At that moment, she forgot the exhausting three-day journey from Los Angeles to the Philippines via Hawaii, Tokyo, and Hong Kong. Her head was already swimming with the sights and sounds of the Orient, all so different from Latin America. At last, she was about to be introduced to Flora Belle's "family" in the Philippines.

After the confusing ordeal of immigration and customs formalities, she emerged from the arrival area with her baggage to be engulfed in the enthusiastic embrace of Flora Belle, a group of excited Filipinos, and the Manila missionary family, the Wayne Wrights. Suddenly, she found herself almost smothered in garlands of sweet-smelling flowers, the traditional Filipino way of saying welcome.

Flora Belle, never at a loss for words, expressed their mutual sentiments, her voice barely audible above the airport noise. "I can't believe you're really here. I have to pinch myself to make sure I'm not dreaming!"

Flora Belle exclaimed about Daisy's white hair, and Daisy remarked with unbelief in her voice, "Look at you! I never thought I would see you so fat! Remember how we always thought of you as the skinny one and me as the stout one?"

Amidst the excited chatter of the welcoming party, she was hustled into the waiting mission vehicle which made its way through the crowded streets of Manila, one of the bustling cities of the Far East. After weaving precariously through the traffic

133

for more than an hour, Daisy decided she was glad she would not be living in the city. Home was to be on the island of Mindanao where Flora Belle was in charge of the Bible school.

After a few days in Manila, Flora Belle and Daisy flew to Mindanao. Daisy found herself settling into life on the campus in Kabakan amidst the happy sounds of nearly a hundred young people going about their duties. She was impressed with the beauty of the Bible school campus. After the cramped plantel in Chiclayo with almost no shrubbery or trees, the acres of lovely green grass, beautiful trees, and flower-bordered pathways of her new home seemed like a tropical paradise. The administration building, dorms, faculty homes, library, and dining room were well-placed with a large tabernacle in the center. Daisy found their second floor mission home spacious and airy, more than adequate for two single ladies.

Flora Belle was known as "Mother" to everyone, students and pastors alike. When she explained to the students that Daisy had been "Mama" to her Peruvian family, they adopted that name for her. From that time on, they were known as the two mothers, culturally very correct for older women in the Philippines.

Daisy found the Philippine customs a mixture of oriental with Spanish and American overtones. Most of the names and religious vocabulary were Spanish, inherited from colonial days under Spain. She found herself straining to untangle the jumble of the new language which sounded like Spanish, but conversations made no sense because all the rest was a "foreign" language to her. English was the educational and business language, compliments of the Americans who controlled the islands for the first half of the twentieth century. But "bamboo" English sounded almost as foreign as their native language, sometimes requiring translation.

With tips from Flora Belle, it didn't take long for Mama Daisy to become a part of the school life just as if she had always been there. She easily slipped into her duties as teacher and school nurse and before long, adopted "bamboo" English as her own. As always, her heart burned with zeal to impart spiritual truths to the young people, and to see them become effective workers for the Lord.

How could I have dreamed of all the beautiful scenery I have seen; of the wonderful people that I have met, who have insisted that their home is mine, and they mean it; the thrill of seeing people come to the Lord and be born again;

> *and then watch them grow in grace. And then the most*
> *thrilling of all, to have the privilege of training some of these*
> *for the ministry.*

After the excitement of Daisy's arrival, Flora Belle slumped into her usual go-when-you-have-to-and-go-to-bed-when-you-don't routine. She was exhausted from the demands of her work and sick from problems resulting from her illness of twenty years earlier. Added to that was a severe back problem caused from many long hours spent bumping over rough roads in trucks or jeeps. Flora Belle thought furloughs were a waste of time, so hers was long overdue.

Daisy decided her biggest challenge would be to keep Flora Belle from destroying herself with her all-consuming sense of faithfulness to duty. She always gave more than one hundred percent of her physical and emotional energy to everything she did. Daisy adopted the role of guardian of Flora Belle's health, insisting that she slow down and take care of herself. Once more she became a "Popish" nurse, saying no to demands upon time and strength on behalf of her dear friend and co-worker. This was to be her assignment from the Lord for the rest of her life, a wonderfully fulfilling one for Daisy who needed to give of herself in service to be happy.

Daisy and Flora Belle had a long-cherished plan in mind when Daisy came to spend that year in the Philippines, supposedly Flora Belle's last before retirement. They both had an insatiable desire to see the missionary work in many other countries of the world. Tentative arrangements were made to go home by way of Southeast Asia, Africa, and Europe, completing a trip around the world for both of them. Flora Belle would pay all expenses above what the home board would normally pay for her return home, and since Daisy was there as a Gospel Corps worker (a volunteer paying her own way), they considered the trip to be perfectly legitimate.

Having their plans upset by new challenges in the work was nothing new for the them. And it happened again. Flora Belle was asked to fill a desperate need in the Bible School in Luzon for one more year before going home, and Daisy would be her helper. During that year, Flora Belle's health deteriorated further, requiring major surgery. Her Wesleyan Filipino doctor placed a strong prohibition on any strenuous activity or rough travel.

At the conclusion of that year, they were to be home in time for Flora Belle to speak for the Wesleyan Women's quadrennial general convention. For good measure, they were asked by the general secretary of world missions to visit Indonesia, a trip which the doctor approved provided she promised not to ride in ox carts or jeeps. The trip around the world which had already become very doubtful for health reasons, was now completely out of the question.

> *Right now, Flora Belle and I are in Manila processing our papers for going to Indonesia. We are almost in a daze, it has come about so suddenly. Of course, we had planned on visiting our missionaries there before going to the States, but thought we might have longer in this part of the world. Bro. Ermal Wilson came from Indonesia . . . and wants us to be sure to visit them before going to the States.*
>
> *We will spend three weeks in Indonesia and be back here for graduation on April 20, district conference and Philippine National Conference. Following that is National Youth Congress. All these will be held on our Rosales campus. Then we will leave later that week.*

Miraculously, all the plans were fulfilled in spite of Flora Belle's fragile health. The visit to Indonesia brought encouragement to the Pantangans who were valiantly carrying on alone. Their report to the Philippine church leaders and to the world missions department in the United States prepared the way for additional missionaries in the years ahead.

Their travels ended in Marion, Indiana, where the international headquarters of The Wesleyan Church was located. Merger of The Pilgrim Holiness Church and The Wesleyan Methodist Church had resulted in the formation of The Wesleyan Church in 1968 while Flora Belle was in the Philippines. As always, Daisy and she wanted to be as near the center of activity of the world missions department as possible. They both intended to keep busy in deputation as long as the department and health would allow. The Marion area became home for the two veteran missionary ladies for the next year and a half.

Corrective surgery for Flora Belle soon after their arrival in Marion kept them at home, but not for long. As soon as she was permitted by the doctor, the two were on the road again speaking in conventions and visiting friends. Flora Belle was the driver of their comfortable car and Daisy was the navigator, planning their routes of travel and keeping them on the right highways. For entertainment over the long boring miles, Daisy counted telephone poles if there were any, or cattle in the fields, or red trucks passing by.

Daisy called this her second retirement and Flora Belle's first, but before they could even settle down, word of new challenges came. Appeals for help from Indonesia via the Philippine Provisional General Conference opened new doors of service.

> *We have enjoyed our cozy mobile home, but Flora Belle says that she is a "tropical baby" and longs for warmer climes.*
>
> *At General Board meeting in November, Flora Belle and I were appointed as associate missionaries to Indonesia for two years, pending medical clearance. Which won't be hard to get. Flora Belle's doctor has already said that he will clear her. I go to our family doctor here next week. It will take a little time to get our visas . . . maybe by the middle of March!*

Excitement reigned in the mobile home as the two ladies bound for Indonesia began to contemplate the trip. Why not make their round-the-world tour now, while they were both able and it could become a part of the trip to Indonesia? They gave a list of twenty-four countries throughout Europe, Africa, the Middle East, and Asia to the travel agent, and the itinerary was made. Much to their delight, they discovered that the stopovers would add almost nothing to their expenses. Once again, they were filled with praise that God was giving them one more bonus blessing to crown their long years of service for Him.

The two septuagenarians were like teenagers on a long holiday as they visited some of the great historical landmarks throughout Europe. They were equally enthralled with some of the geographic wonders of the world such as Stonehenge. Both women had a deep appreciation for art, natural wonders, music, and great architecture, so the famous museums, opera houses, and cathedrals of Europe were on their itinerary. They saw the Pyramids and Sphinx in Egypt and the Taj Mahal in India. Exquisite small souvenirs were carefully chosen to remind them of the grand sights.

One day during that trip, they waited for a bus on a street corner in Amsterdam in the Netherlands. Flora Belle sat on her portable stool attached to a cane while Daisy stood beside her, blue eyes dancing with excitement in a face framed with unruly white curls escaping from the soft bun on top of her head. A curious gentleman, amused at the strange sight of two rather

plump older tourists obviously enthralled with their surroundings, paused to ask where they were from. When they told him
they were from America, he laughed and said, "Oh, the original
Bobsey twins, no?" And that's what they were to each other
ever after.

The highlight of that trip was their visit to South Africa and
Swaziland where Flora Belle had lived as a child while her parents were missionaries. Her father died and was buried in South
Africa while on an evangelistic visit there many years later.
Daisy shared Flora Belle's deep sense of fulfillment as they
returned to her childhood home in Swaziland, the mission station her parents pioneered more than sixty years before.

Their long journey ended in Indonesia in November 1973
where Daisy and Flora Belle worked for more than three years, at
first helping the Pantangans with their pioneer church planting
project in Bandung. Then they started a Bible School in their
living room where they trained the first Indonesian Wesleyan
pastor. Through their inspiration and leadership, the center of
the work was located in Magelang in Central Java. The small
Bible school beginning later developed into Wesleyan Bible
College, a government-recognized institution located on a beautiful campus.

> *This is an interesting island — Java is about the size of
> the state of Illinois, but has over 90 million people on it!
> People are everywhere! The majority of these people are
> Muslims, but not too fanatic in most parts of the island.
> Most of them have never heard that Jesus Christ came to
> save men from their sins. Someone has said that if a mis-
> sionary couple could preach in a different village five times a
> week, 20 times a month, 240 times a year, and had 1,000
> people in every service, it would still take more than 100
> years to preach once to everyone on this island.*
>
> *Magelang is a smaller city at the very geographical cen-
> ter of this island, with many small villages (10,000 popula-
> tion each) surrounding. It is to these people that we hope to
> be able to carry the gospel.*

Daisy wrote about some of their personal experiences in this
exotic tropical, Muslim country.

> *If you are going to learn a new language, I recommend
> that you do so while young! In the Philippines I was frus-
> trated at first with the "bamboo English," often needing an*

interpreter. But when we came to Indonesia the situation was different. We really needed to try to learn a new language — at our age it is much easier to forget! But how can you expect more of 70-plus oldsters?

We learned that single women, no matter how old, should always respond to the question, "Are you married?" with the hopeful reply, "Not yet." In Indonesian, of course. We could always remember to say that correctly!

Three weeks ago I was in a little accident. There is so much to thank the Lord for, since it could have been so much worse. It had been raining, and the tricycle (a man-powered rickshaw) I was riding in went out of control on a slight incline and turned over. I was dumped out on my hands and knees on the street. My forehead and my thigh got the blow, but no broken bones, no bruises on my arm. My glasses were bent but not broken. Two of our young men were riding in a tricycle behind, and they came running. There was no traffic on what usually has heavy traffic. An ambulance came by, which is not seen on that street as a rule, and I went to First Aid at the nearby Catholic hospital — against my wishes. I've had no pain after the first blow, and the black is almost all gone.

The Indonesia years were happy and fruitful, but they took their toll on both Daisy and Flora Belle. They felt released to return home to retire once more after Robert and Julia Smith, former co-workers from the Philippines, arrived to help the Pantangans. Their homeward trip completed their tour around the world, taking them through the Philippines, Korea, and Japan.

I had my 77th birthday while in Japan, and they told me that is a special year, because the characters for 77 also mean "happiness" — so this is my "happiness" year. They gave me special favors, too!
Flora Belle's brother and his wife, and her sister and her husband met us at the L.A. airport. Then I went on to San Diego . . . spoke in several churches while there. At Skyline church the evening I spoke there, the pastor asked 4 young men to come, and he gave each a dollar bill, and then sent them out through the congregation to get as many dollars as they could while everyone sang, "Happy birthday, Daisy."

He had them sing slowly!

We bought a car in California and my sister helped us to drive it across the country to Indianapolis. We spoke in two churches on Sunday and then came on to Marion. It has been 5 months since we left Indonesia, and we still haven't arrived — that is, to where we will make home. We are asking the Lord to make His will plain to us.

This was Daisy's third and final retirement and Flora Belle's second. Step by step, God revealed His beautiful plan for them, a plan which required only one serious adjustment. This time, He called them to live among "old" people!

Chapter 16

Finally, Retirement!

Home at Last

"No eye has seen, no ear has heard, no mind has conceived what God has prepared for those who love him" — but God has revealed it to us by his Spirit (I Corinthians 2:9-10 NIV).

The early morning quietness was broken by the song of birds awakening to the first pink streaks of dawn in the eastern sky behind the cozy retirement home in Brooksville, Florida. A few moments later, the morning dew, lighted by shafts of golden sunlight filtering through the pine trees, sparkled on red hibiscus beside the windows of the Florida room. Daisy, always a morning person, sat with her Bible in her lap, musing about the goodness of God as she looked out on the majestic serenity of the new day.

Since moving into their home in Brooksville, there were many mornings in which to savor memories of the past as she waited for Flora Belle, a night person, to awaken. In those quiet moments, she enjoyed reading through her journals and adding clippings she found among her treasured papers. Her picture albums grew thicker, too, as she sorted through the hundreds of pictures taken over the years, reminders of the joys and pains, struggles and triumphs of the past.

During one of those mornings, she found a yellowed scrap of paper in a trunk that had remained unopened for many years. On it was a poem she had copied when she was a child of eight. The penciled lines were faded, but the message spoke to her again as she faced the challenges of each new day. She pasted it inside the cover of one of her most recent journals to be an encouragement for "now."

You cannot change yesterday, that is clear,

Or begin tomorrow until it is here.
So the only thing that is left for you and me
Is to make today as sweet as can be.

There wasn't much in her yesterdays she would have
changed if she could. They had been rich with both delightful
and painful experiences woven together by her Heavenly Father
into the tapestry of her life. Now, after nearly eight decades of
living according to his plan, contentment reigned in her heart
and beautified her countenance.

Daisy saw the hand of God clearly at work since she and
Flora Belle returned from Indonesia. Their lovely home on missionary row in Brooksville was one of His gifts to them.
Although it was much the same as all the others provided by the
department of world missions for retired missionaries, Daisy and
Flora Belle had been allowed to make some modifications at
their own expense. It bore the stamp of their insistence on fru-
gality, but it also reflected their ability to plan for convenience
and comfort. It was bright and spacious inside, and almost
maintenance free.

The house that the Department of World Missions built
for us is lovely. We have a living room, dining room,
kitchen, Florida room, two bedrooms, a den, one full bath,
and one three quarter, and a carport.
Our house is a little like a museum, because for the first
time, we are able to unpack our souvenirs and keepsakes
from all the places we have been in the world.

Daisy enjoyed the quiet, caring atmosphere of Wesleyan
Village, a retirement community primarily for Wesleyans. The
church in the village had wonderful pastors and was filled every
Sunday with people much like themselves. Besides that, the best
preachers of the holiness movement came to minister at the
Bible conferences and camps held during the year. The yearly
highlight for them was the exciting three-day missionary convention scheduled for the Thanksgiving holidays.

Daisy and Flora Belle took great delight in sharing the stories
of their lives with friends and loved ones who came to visit.
They were illustrated with curios taken from the shelves that
lined two walls of their living room — exquisite carvings, minia-
ture characters, beautiful china, even antique artifacts from the
Inca tombs in Peru.

One of the more difficult aspects of life since coming to

Florida was their gradually deteriorating health. Flora Belle suffered a slight stroke in April, 1979, partially paralyzing one side of her body for a while. Daisy explained what happened to the doctor, adding that she thought they might be trying to do too much. They had traveled over seven thousand miles from January until April that year, speaking in more than fifty churches. The doctor ordered complete rest and medications for Flora Belle. He began his instructions by exclaiming, "Have you girls ever heard about retirement?"

A few weeks later, Daisy went to the doctor with her own problems.

> *Last month the doctor found that I am a borderline diabetic. I also had some trouble with my heart suddenly racing and skipping beats. However, the doctor says its not serious and the medication he gave seems to have corrected the problem. Again we thank the Lord. The doctor wants us to take services again, though not so strenuous. He feels we need the challenge.*

Daisy was glad to be free from the tyranny of difficult schedules and fully enjoyed her "retired" status. But Flora Belle, always restless, longed to be with the people she loved in faraway places. While she recovered from the stroke, she dreamed constantly of making just one more trip to the Philippines and Indonesia. Daisy who loved to travel, dreamed with her. They wrote a joint letter to friends in 1981 about their activities and hopes for the future.

> *Since being "retired" (I am allergic to that word) we go to meetings by invitation, and it is such a joy to meet so many who are truly interested in missions. Daisy will tell you about the meetings.*
>
> *The complaint here in Wesleyan Village is that we don't stay at home. The truth is that in the nearly four years since we left Indonesia we have been away from home much longer than at home. We left Jakarta on March 3, 1977 and arrived here to retire November 5th, doing some deputation in Kansas and other places along the way. And since then we have had the privilege of visiting many churches all over the eastern United States, making visits upon request for missionary services and conventions. We also had a wonderful trip to Eau Claire, Wisconsin, for a convention.*

> *Flora Belle tells people that since we are called "the girls" here we had to represent the youth of Wesleyan Village at the International Wesleyan Youth Convention in Urbana, Illinois, two years ago. Of course our main reason for going was to see our children from the places where we have served. The same at the Wesleyan World Fellowship last May in Marion, followed by the General Conference in Indianapolis in June. How we did enjoy visiting with them! The trouble is that it doesn't help our homesickness.*

By the end of the year, Flora Belle was sufficiently recovered to drive their car and take some meetings again. One of those assignments was the junior youth camp for the Georgia district in 1980. The young people loved the two grandmotherly women who told them wonderful stories and showed them many exciting things from far-off lands. And Daisy and Flora Belle loved the young people.

After that experience they read together in their devotions about Barzillai.

> *Recently in family devotions we were reading II Samuel 19 about Barzillai, and it says, "Now Barzillai was a very aged man, even 80 years old."*
>
> *Flora Belle said, "See what the Bible says about 80-years-olds!" But I (Daisy) am not that old, because I still can taste, and I can still enjoy singing.*

God allowed some help for the homesickness in 1982 with a trip to Indonesia and the Philippines which lasted six months. Their stay in Indonesia was limited to only three weeks because of visa restrictions. The rest of the time was spent in the Philippines visiting five of the six districts where they were with their "children" on four islands. But once again, Flora Belle's physical condition necessitated their return home sooner than they had planned.

Back home in Brooksville, a series of illnesses finally made it necessary for Flora Belle to be cared for in a nursing home. During the four long months of that first nursing home experience, Daisy's lifetime of faithfulness to duty was demonstrated again as she visited Flora Belle every day except one. She wrote to her friends about the struggles of those days.

> *Two songs have been such a blessing these weeks, "How Firm a Foundation" and*

> *A wonderful Saviour is Jesus my Lord.*
> *He taketh my burden away.*
> *He holdeth me up, and I shall not be moved,*
> *He giveth me strength for each day!*

> *And on through the chorus.*

> *Flora Belle is so pitiful, but on the whole she is quite cheerful. She talks a lot some days, but nothing makes sense — we can't even guess what she is trying to say. She walks with help and has to be fed. She is "gone" and yet still here in body. Some days she seems to recognize me and some friends, but her memory span is so short that the recognition doesn't last long, sometimes only seconds.*

In late November, God granted Daisy another miracle. Flora Belle suddenly became coherent, and her ability to take care of herself returned. Daisy was jubilant, and the doctor was amazed.

Their little retirement home was happier for Daisy when Flora Belle was allowed to return.

> *We are praising the Lord for his special hand on Flora Belle. She is at home and has her memory and ability to speak and to do for herself again. Our doctor was so thrilled on November 2nd (1983) when she recognized him after over 3 months that she didn't know who he was. He says that this cannot be explained at all medically. It is a miracle. He didn't expect she would ever improve. I brought her home to stay on the 8th of December. The shine is back in her eyes.*

Daisy and Flora Belle made their last trip together in June of 1984 to the Festival of Missions and General Conference. This time, they made the journey with the Reverend and Mrs. Arthur Bray, pastor of their church in Brooksville.

> *How Flora Belle and I did enjoy our "family" from far off places. She stood the trip well. It was really good for her. We were sorry that all of you weren't able to attend especially the Festival of Missions.*

As retirement years passed, Daisy and Flora Belle were more and more confined to their home in Brooksville. All that Daisy had become through the years was more apparent as she lived one day at a time, patiently, lovingly making life as sweet as she could for both of them. In March 1986, Flora Belle suffered a stroke and heart attack, and the doctor gave no hope of recovery. Through the help of Ken Horton, their young friend who had come to visit them from Orlando, she arranged a second time for Flora Belle to be transferred from the hospital to Eastbrooke Nursing Home in Brooksville.

Perhaps the most terrifying experience of Daisy's whole life occurred on the way home. As they passed the high school, a sixteen-year-old girl drove out from the school directly in front of their car. In the collision, Daisy hit the windshield, and she was knocked unconscious. She suffered a concussion, a long gash on the forehead and jaw, and other bruises. Miraculously, there were no broken bones.

After five days in the hospital, she was allowed to go home, but not to see Flora Belle. Six weeks after the accident, she was taken to Tampa for special surgery to remove blood from the brain. In less than three weeks after surgery she was her old self again, although she was completely bald. It had been necessary to shave off all her long white hair for the surgery. Later, she wrote to her friends about the accident, especially the hair!

> *My hair is growing fast and seems much heavier than before. A lady here brought me a wig that she had gotten for her mother at Goodwill for fifty cents. It looks as though it were my own. I've had to be introduced quite a few times. I've had a lot of fun over it.*

While Daisy was passing through her deep valley, Flora Belle was moved to the nursing home, and was finally told by the doctor about her friend's troubles. When Daisy was able to visit Flora Belle, she seemed not to have any sense of the passing of time since Daisy had last been to see her. Those weeks seemed like an eternity to Daisy.

> *When I went to see her she recognized me, wig and all. When I had gotten half way into her room, she cried and held out her arms. I've seen her several times, and she has recognized me each time. Her memory span is very short, but she seems to be happy in spite of the fact that things aren't as nice as she wishes.*

Those several weeks of traumatic events launched Daisy

upon a whole new way of life. After seventeen years of living and working with Flora Belle, and of being the constant guardian of her health, she found her hands empty. God's assignment seemed to have come to an end, except for visits to the nursing home. There was so much to be thankful for, but also a deep sadness to cope with until God finally lifted the clouds of loneliness.

In a few weeks, God sent along another delightful person whom she had known for many years, younger and totally different from Flora Belle. Miss Lena Brown, missionary from Africa, needed a retirement home, and Daisy needed someone to live with her. It was a perfect solution to both of their problems. Once again, Daisy's Heavenly Father did more for her than she could have imagined.

Daisy never stopped being concerned about her "family" in other lands. She wrote to one of her "children" in Indonesia, almost a summary of her life and the lessons she was still learning from God.

> *I've learned so much more about the Lord! I've learned to know Him better. What a marvelous God we serve. He is so loving and caring. It seems as though I've just gotten a peek into His greatness. Things that I've known all my life, I find seem to become more real as though I hadn't even seen the fact before.*
>
> *I realized in a much greater way that the Lord is with us now. Then the fact of eternity! How sensible is God's plan. The short span of our life in comparison. How wonderfully whatever time of suffering we've had (I've had so little) melts into eternity, and then there is no suffering at all — forever.*
>
> *Whatever comes to make us more conscious of our relationship to God is a blessing, not only to us as individuals, but to those we encounter.*
>
> *And then the blessing of song! Even in the midst of severe accusation, God gives songs in the night and all the day long. Even the songs that I hear down in my heart are such an encouragement. "Lord, lift me up and let me stand, By faith on heaven's table land."*
>
> *And the precious promises! Learn them. Underline them. Use them daily. God will give you His blessing and help in the midst of hard places. "Fear not, for I am with thee. Be not dismayed."*

Early in 1987, Daisy went on a journey again, this time to visit her brother, Billy, and his wife in Tulsa, Oklahoma. From there, she and Billy went together to visit their sister, Elva, and her family in southern California. She revelled in the joys of seeing loved ones and dear friends of other years back in her old California "home."

Daisy spent the last month of her life with the Wrights at a Wesleyan Women International convention in South Carolina and in Indianapolis. She was still the same sweet, happy person, eager to be a part of all that was going on. Her eyes shone with delight and approval as she visited the new international head-quarters of her church.

When she was asked to accompany the Wrights to two weekend missionary conventions, she went and even participated. In one service, she held the children spellbound as she told her "falling-off-the-horse" story.

In another, Daisy was asked to give a testimony and challenge to the young people present. It was the same message she had been giving young people since her very first missionary deputation meetings almost sixty years before. Only now, it flowed out of a lifetime of experience.

If God calls you to be a missionary, consider it a special favor from Him. No matter what work He gives you to do, do it with your whole heart. Some folks feel sorry for us, but that is not necessary, because we get so many extras from the Lord. Even what may seem like a sacrifice never turns out to be one, because of what He gives. God has done so much for us, and here in this world is the only place where we can show our trust in Him.

Ten days after Daisy flew back to Brooksville, God took her to himself quickly with minimal suffering, the result of two heart attacks spaced several days apart. He must have been saying, "You have shown me that you trusted me there in your earthly home long enough. It's time now to come to the home I have prepared for you."

A long life, well-lived, came to an end. The spiritual foundations of early years stood the tests of time and toils. The missionary character remained constant and clear from continent to continent. Unselfish devotion to her Lord and His people did not change though circumstances often did. Treasures laid up in heaven are now hers to enjoy for all eternity.

Scores of men and women who called her "Mama" are following her example, faithful in service to God and the church. They are today's pastors, leaders, and laymen in all the lands where she served.

A life so radiantly transparent and quietly consistent as Daisy's is rarely seen among the ranks of God's good people. The greatest of all her remarkable achievements was the manner in which she modeled the servant nature of Jesus. With a heart full of love, she lived for him by ministering to others wherever she was.